Nuts! Nuts! Nuts!

by

Ann Mason Norton

Published by Handy Andy Industries, Inc.
Box 2456
Jonesboro, Ark. 72401

International Standard Book Number—0-918544-49-1

Printed in the United States of America
WIMMER BROTHERS FINE PRINTING & LITHOGRAPHY
Memphis, Tennessee 38118

"Cookbooks of Distinction"™

FORWARD

Nut meats are highly nutritious and have been an essential part of man's diet for centuries.

During our travels around the country my husband and I have discovered that various nuts are eaten in all parts of the United States and the world but mainly during the holiday season—Thanksgiving to Christmas.

Because nuts can be easily cracked and the nutmeats stored in the freezer, it is the purpose of this book to encourage everyone to use nuts all year round. The high prices of shelled nuts in the grocery store makes it more attractive to buy nuts in the shell when they are plentiful and crack and shell them at one's leisure. With a supply of nutmeats in your freezer, the recipes in this cook book can be made during any season—summer, fall, winter and spring.

A very special "thank you" to Ann and Charles Ford for their hours of help on this book and for being great neighbors. A word of appreciation for the friends whose recipes I used in this book and for the friends whose encouragement has meant so much.

To Bob, Jr., Kelley Gray and Andy, thank you for letting Mom "work." To Bob, should I thank you for thinking up work for me to do?

A big "thank you" to everyone who uses this cook book. We hope you enjoy it.

CONTENTS

In a

Nutshell

In a

Nutshell

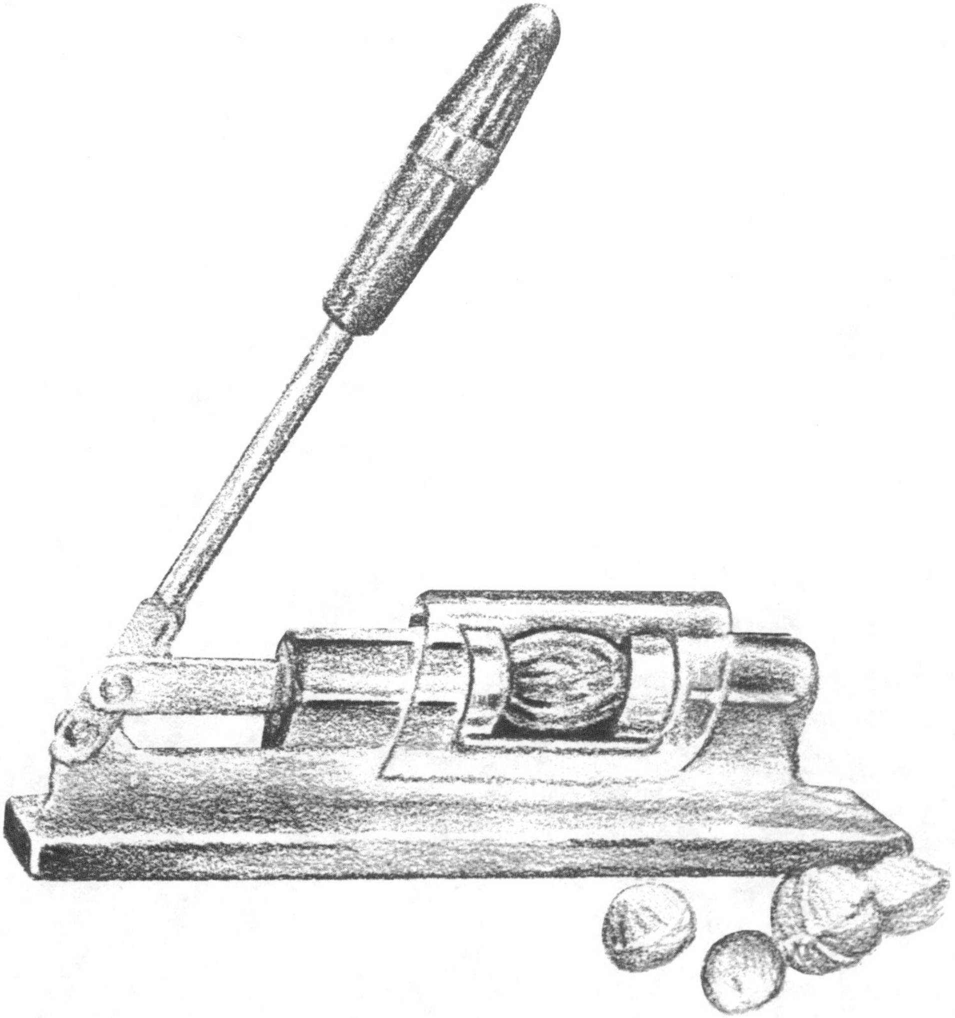

IN A NUTSHELL

Nuts are one of the oldest foods used by birds, animals and man. A great snack, nuts are a high energy food and are eaten in every country of the world. Nuts give food good smell, flavor, crispness, tenderness and garnish.

The sweet almond we eat and use in cooking has been used since the earliest recorded times. Almonds are used in desserts, pastry, souffles, liquer, sauces, cakes, candy, cookies, vegetables and with meat, fish and chicken. Whole, halved, slivered, sliced or chopped, almonds can be blanched or used plain, salted or toasted.

The black walnut is the toughest of all nuts to crack, but contains a high quality nut meat that is sought after by many people. Black walnuts retain their own distinct taste after cooking and are used in ice cream, breads, cakes and candy.

Brazil nuts are indeed a product of Brazil and are imported into the United States. Used for breads, cakes, cookies, candy, salads, appetizers, desserts, ice cream and main course dishes, Brazil nuts can be sliced, chopped, ground and buttered, salted, roasted or candied.

Growing wild and not marketed commercially, butternuts are found from the Eastern United States to the Dakotas. The shells are hard to crack and the nut meats must be picked over carefully to remove the bitter pieces of the inner walls. Butternuts are tasty in cakes and breads.

Chestnuts have been used since ancient times and are the only nuts that are actually eaten as a vegetable. Not as plentiful in North America as they once were, most of our chestnuts are imported from Europe. Excellent in stews and stuffings, they can be used in gravies and sauces as well as pickled. Chestnuts can be used in cakes, puddings and ice cream.

The coconut is the fruit of the palm tree and is the world's largest nut. Coconut may be used fresh but is also available grated or shredded, canned or frozen, sweetened or unsweetened. Shredded or grated, coconut is excellent in or with desserts, cakes, creams, pies and a great number of sweets.

English walnuts have been used in every way imaginable, plain and fancy. California is the world's leader in English walnut production. Plentiful, they are perhaps the world's most used nut. They can be substituted in any recipe calling for pecans or almonds.

The American northwest has become a major producer of filberts or hazelnuts as they are called in some parts of the country. A delicious nut, filberts can be roasted, blanched or unblanched, and toasted, salted or candied. They are used in candy, baked goods, salads, and breads, and with meat, fish and game.

Some people find the hickory nut the best flavored of all nuts. Not marketed commercially, this native American nut is in very limited supply. When found hickory nuts are extremely difficult to crack because of their hard shell. Hickory nuts are used in breads, cakes and pastries.

Native to Australia macadamia nuts have been grown in Hawaii for about 100 years and are now being grown in California. A very thick, hard shell covers a delectable nutmeat that can be eaten raw but is usually roasted and often salted. Macadamia nuts can be used in cakes, cookies, puddings and breads. Hopefully, macadamia nuts will become more widely marketed in the next few years.

The peanut is not a nut, per se, but is related to the bean and the pea. Because of its popularity and nut-like qualities, the peanut is included in this cook book. Peanuts are readily available in the shell, raw, salted or unsalted. Peanuts are well-known for their high food value and can be buttered, salted or prepared in any number of ways.

The pecan is a native American nut. Pecan trees grow profusely in the southern United States and as far north as Virginia and Indiana. Suitable to use with almost all other food, pecans are used in desserts, candy, cakes, fruit cups, salads, snacks, vegetables and main course dishes. Use them raw, salted, roasted, spiced, sugared and chilied, halved, chopped or ground.

The pistachio may be the oldest known nut in the world. Major pistachio production has been in the middle east, but California is becoming a major producer of pistachios and in future years we may be seeing more of these delicious nuts. Pistachios are used in stuffings, patés, breads, cakes and other desserts. They can be used raw or salted.

In the recipes in this book use pecans, butternuts, hickory nuts, macadamia nuts and walnuts raw unless stated otherwise. Blanche almonds, peanuts, Brazil nuts, filberts and pistachios before using in recipes unless stated otherwise. Chestnuts must be shelled and skinned before using. Coconut can be fresh, canned or frozen, but use it raw unless recipe calls for toasted coconut.

Any nut can be substituted for another in any recipe. Flavor will change but substitution sometimes makes a recipe better. Use what you have on hand.

GATHERING NUTS

At least one type of nut tree will grow in every state of the United States south of Alaska. More than one type of nut tree will grow in many states. Many people have their own nut trees or have access to trees that grow wild.

Nuts are usually gathered from the ground but can also be harvested by shaking the tree. Nuts taken from the ground often have shed their hulls or, in fact, left their hulls on the tree. If the nuts are still in the hull, removing the hull immediately is important to both the flavor and color of the nut meat.

The black walnut is the toughest nut to hull. Some people use an old fashioned corn sheller. Others spread the nuts on a concrete drive and drive over them til the hulls are mashed. Whatever method one uses it is best to wear a pair of gloves or the stain will be with you awhile.

After hulling the nuts, the nuts in their shells should be washed thoroughly. Next spread the nuts in a single layer on a clean surface and allow them to dry for several weeks. Turn the nuts every day or so to be sure they are drying evenly.

If nuts have been on the ground for awhile without the hull, chances are they are dryed or cured when you gather them. Crack one or two and taste them. The flavor will tell you whether you should store them in a cool dry place for awhile or whether you can proceed with shelling.

BUYING NUTS IN THE SHELL

Buy nuts in the shell from your grocer, a roadside stand or a reputable catalogue company. Handy Andy has a gift assortment on the market that contains one Handy Andy nutcracker and several pounds of grade A-1 nuts in the shell. Ask your favorite grocer or retailer for help in finding nuts in the shell. Generally they are available in most parts of the country from October through December.

Be sure shells are clean and free of cracks. When buying a coconut, look for "eyes" that are not moldy. Choose a coconut that feels heavy and sounds full of liquid when shaken.

Below is the approximate amount of nutmeats you will get from 1 pound of nuts in the shell:

1 pound almonds	1¼ cups nutmeats
1 pound Brazil nuts	1½ cups nutmeats
1 pound black walnuts	1 cup
1 pound butternuts	3 to 4 cups nutmeats
1 pound chestnuts	2½ cups nutmeats
1 pound English walnuts	1⅔ cups nutmeats
1 pound filberts (hazelnuts)	1½ cups nutmeats
1 pound macadamia nuts	1½ cups nutmeats
1 pound peanuts	2¼ cups nutmeats
1 pound pistachios	4 cups nutmeats
1 medium coconut	3 to 4 cups meat

STORING NUTS

Buy or gather nuts in the shell in the fall when they are plentiful. Stored in a cool, dry place, nuts in the shell will last for about one year. Shelled and put in an airtight container or plastic bag in the freezer, nuts will last indefinitely. Whole nuts and whole halves retain a better flavor than bits and pieces of nuts.

To use frozen nutmeats, simply remove the amount of nutmeats needed from the container and chop, slice or prepare them as called for in your recipe. Nutmeats do not need to be defrosted before adding to a recipe. They can be refrozen.

CRACKING NUTS

You can buy nuts already shelled, but it saves money to crack and shell your own. Some nuts can be cracked by squeezing two together in the palm of your hand. The wear and tear on the hand as well as the broken nut meats makes this tedious.

Help is available. The Handy Andy nutcracker cracks soft and medium shell nuts such as almonds, Brazil nuts, English walnuts, filberts (hazelnuts) and pecans. Simply slide the shield toward the back of the nutcracker, screw the threaded ram with the nut in place til the handle is just above the leverage point as shown. This is about a 45° angle. Slide the shield to cover the nut and keep the hulls from scattering. Pull the handle down just til the ends of the nut explode. Adjusted correctly the Handy Andy will give you whole halves or whole nutmeats almost every time. Mounting brackets are available to mount Handy Andy on a work bench or wall to make cracking a lot of nuts at one time simple and fast. If similar size nuts are cracked in succession you need adjust the threaded ram only when changing sizes.

The Handy Andy Hard Shell Nutcracker cracks all nuts, but was designed for the hard shelled black walnut, hickory nut, macadamia nut and butternut. Mount the brackets on a work table following the diagram in the box. Put the nutcracker in the brackets, put the handle in place and slide the shield toward the handle end of the nutcracker. Position the nut so pressure will be on the ends of the nut. Slide the shield over nut and turn the handle til the nut cracks. The shield will contain the nut meat as well as the hulls.

Men and children like to use Handy Andy. Let them crack the nuts and put them in a grocery sack. Try to crack the same size nuts at one time so nutcracker does not have to be adjusted so often. Nuts can be shelled while watching TV or relaxing.

Coconuts can be easily cracked, also. Pierce the "eyes" of the coconut with a screw driver or ice pick and drain off milk. Put the coconut in a 400° oven for 20 minutes. Remove the coconut from oven and tap lightly all over with a hammer to loosen shell. Hit harder with hammer—coconut cracks open with seemingly no effort. Cut off the dark skin.

Be sure to taste fresh coconut before putting it in a recipe. It should taste good and sweet. If not, discard the coconut and milk and proceed with another one. Freeze any left over coconut in an airtight container for use at another time. Recipes in this book can be used with fresh, canned or frozen coconut.

Pistachios have the outer shell removed during the curing process. The inner shell can be easily removed with the fingernail. Simply press peanuts with the thumb and forefinger to open shell and release nuts. Shelling chestnuts is discussed under BLANCHING as both processes are accomplished together.

BLANCHING NUTS

Put shelled almonds in saucepan and cover with cold water. Bring water to a boil, remove from heat and let almonds stand in water 2 to 3 minutes. Drain. Press small end of nut between thrumb and forefinger and slip off skin. Let nuts dry before freezing or using. Blanch about ¼ pound almonds at one time.

Spread filberts (hazelnuts), peanuts or pistachios in a shallow pan. Toast in oven at 350° for 10 minutes or til the skins crack. Cover nuts with boiling water and let stand for 2 minutes. Drain. Rub nuts with rough towel to remove skins.

Place single layer of Brazil nuts in baking pan and cook for ½ hour in 300° oven before cracking. If skins remain after cracking, put nuts in a pan, cover with boiling water and let stand for 5 minutes. Drain. Rub off skin with fingers.

Chestnuts can be shelled and blanched at the same time. With a sharp knife cut a crisscross gash in the shell on the flat side of each chestnut. Do not cut into nutmeat. Put nuts in saucepan and cover with 1 inch boiling water and let stand for 10 minutes. With a slotted spoon lift out 3 or 4 chestnuts at a time and peel off shell and skin.

Recipes in this cook book that call for almonds, filberts, Brazil nuts, peanuts, pistachios and chestnuts are for blanched nuts unless stated otherwise. Pecans, English walnuts, black walnuts, hickory nuts and butternuts never need blanching.

CHOPPING NUTS: If you want large pieces of walnuts or pecans, break them with your fingers. For finer chopped nuts, a chopper consisting of a glass jar with a plastic apparatus on top which contains a chopping mechanism is available in most stores at a low price. For the larger nuts, an onion chopper will work well.

An electric blender will chop nuts, also. Work with a small quantity at a time and regulate the size of the pieces by the length of time you press the "on" switch.

You can chop nuts on a wooden cutting board using a very sharp knife.

GRINDING NUTS: Use a meat grinder with a fine blade, an electric blender or food processor. With the latter two, turn on, then off immediately. Continue processing til nuts are of desired consistency.

SLICING NUTS: Have nuts, blanched or not, at room temperature. On cutting board with a very sharp knife cut nuts crosswise very thinly.

If recipe calls for toasted sliced nuts, toast after slicing. Almonds are often used sliced in a recipe.

SLIVERING NUTS: Have nuts, blanched or not, at room temperature. Cut on wooden cutting board with a sharp heavy knife lengthwise.

If recipe calls for toasted slivered nuts, toast after slivering. Almonds and Brazil nuts are the nuts most often slivered.

FRYING NUTS: Heat 2 cups oil for each quart of nuts. Add nuts and cook over low heat, stirring until brown. Spread on paper towel and sprinkle with salt to taste.

ROASTING NUTS: Roasting is the oldest way of preparing nuts. Blanch almonds, Brazil nuts and filberts if desired. Pecans, walnuts and macadamia nuts do not need blanching. Keep nutmeats unbroken if possible.

Spread nuts in a single layer in oblong pan. Dot with 1 tablespoon butter or oleo for each cup of nuts. Brown in 400° oven, stirring every 5 minutes. Take pecans out of oven as soon as butter sizzles. Do not over-cook—nuts darken as they cool.

Roast macadamia nuts at 275° for 12 to 15 minutes in coconut oil for best results. Spread nuts on paper towels. Salt to taste.

Prick skins of chestnuts, place in single layer in oblong pan and place in 425° oven for 15 to 20 minutes.

To roast peanuts in the shell, spread peanuts on baking sheet and roast at 300° for 30 to 45 minutes, turning the nuts frequently. Let cool.

To roast shelled peanuts, spread the shelled nuts on baking sheet and roast at 300° for 20 to 30 minutes, turning frequently. Taste to tell if they are done. When done the outer skins rub off easily. If nuts are to be used in a recipe, rub off skins. If they are to be ground you may or may not remove the skins depending on the flavor or nature of the recipe.

TOASTING NUTS: Blanch almonds, Brazil nuts and filberts and dry thoroughly. Slice, sliver or chop, if desired, before toasting. Pecans, walnuts, macadamia nuts, hickory nuts and butternuts do not need blanching.

Put nutmeat in single layer in oblong pan. Brown in 350° oven, stirring occasionally. Toast pecans about 5 minutes, other nutmeats about 10 minutes except macadamia nuts. Toast macadamia nuts in 275° oven for 40 to 50 minutes, stirring often.

Spread grated, shredded or chipped coconut on baking sheet and put it in 350° oven for about 10 minutes, stirring frequently. Remove and cool before using unless you are putting toasted coconut in a hot dish.

Toast peanuts and chestnuts as for roasting nuts.

BOILING PEANUTS: Wash raw peanuts in the shell. Add one tablespoon salt to each quart of water and boil peanuts 2½ to 3 hours. They can be eaten immediately or removed from water, dried, then eaten.

CANNING BOILED PEANUTS: Wash raw peanuts in the shell. Put in large kettle, cover with water and bring water to boil. Put peanuts in shell in quart jars and fill jars with boiling water to within ½ inch of top. Add 2 tablespoons salt to each jar. Cook in pressure canner at 10 pounds pressure for 30 minutes. Remove, cool and store.

TINTING COCONUT: Place 1⅓ cups flaked coconut in a clean pint jar. Add a few drops food coloring. Screw on lid. Shake jar til coconut is colored.

GRATING COCONUT: Peel dark skin from coconut. Use a metal grater and grate coconut as you would cheese.

COCONUT MILK

Combine the grated meat of one coconut with the drained natural coconut milk. Place in 325° oven and heat thoroughly. Remove and cool. Strain coconut milk into a cold bowl. Put coconut in several layers of cheesecloth. Fold cloth over coconut meat and twist from both ends, pressing out all liquid. Combine this with the first liquid. If not for immediate use, refrigerate.

If thick cream comes to the top and gets hard, remove hard cream from container and stir to a creamy consistency by adding, little by little, some of the thinner watery residue.

COCONUT SYRUP

1 coconut
4 cups water
3 cups sugar

Grate the coconut. Combine sugar and water in saucepan, boil to thick syrup. Add grated coconut, blend. Reduce heat, simmer til mixture is translucent, about 25 minutes. Cool, pour into sterilized jars, seal.

SPECIAL HELPS

Use plain flour unless recipe calls for another kind.

Use unsifted flour unless otherwise stated in recipe.

Corn syrup is light corn syrup unless recipe calls for dark corn syrup.

Use pecans and walnuts raw unless stated otherwise in recipe.

Blanche almonds, Brazil nuts, filberts and pistachios in recipe unless stated otherwise.

Pecans, English walnuts and almonds are the most common nuts used in cooking. Each can be substituted for the other in most recipes.

Appetizers

Appetizers

BARBECUED PECANS

2 tablespoons butter or oleo
¼ cup Worcestershire
1 tablespoon catsup
2 dashes Tabasco
4 cups pecan halves
Salt

In large saucepan melt butter. Add Worcestershire, catsup and Tabasco. Stir in nuts. Spoon into oblong pan, spread evenly. Put in 400° oven for 20 minutes, stirring frequently. Drain on paper towel. Sprinkle with salt. Store in airtight container.

BRAZIL NUT CHIPS

Shell Brazil nuts, cover with cold water. Bring slowly to a boil. Simmer 3 minutes. Cool. Cut in thin strips lengthwise. Spread in shallow pan. Dot with butter, using 1 tablespoon to each cup of nuts. Sprinkle with salt. Bake 15 minutes at 350°, stirring occasionally. Drain on paper towel.

BUTTERED PECANS

12 cups pecan halves
1 stick butter or oleo
Salt

Place pecans in pan in 250° oven for 30 minutes. Dot pecans with butter. Stir twice letting pecans get greasy. Sprinkle with salt generously. Continue to stir and salt often for at least one hour or until butter is absorbed.

CURRIED PEANUTS

1 pound salted peanuts
3 or 4 tablespoons curry powder

Preheat oven to 300°. Put peanuts in shallow pan. Bake for 15 to 20 minutes, stirring occasionally to prevent burning. Remove, while hot, stir in curry powder. Cool. Store in airtight tin.

CURRIED ALMONDS

2 cups blanched almonds
¼ cup butter or oleo
2 teaspoons seasoned salt
1 tablespoon curry powder
Salt

Bake nuts at 300° for 25 minutes. In saucepan, combine butter, seasoned salt and curry powder. Simmer until blended. Pour over nuts, roast 20 more minutes. Drain on paper towels. Salt to taste.

DEVILED NUTS

½ pound blanched almonds or pecans
1½ tablespoons butter or oleo
Salt, paprika, Worcestershire and Tabasco to taste

Over low heat, fry nuts in butter til golden brown, stirring constantly. Coat well with seasoning. Cool. Store in tins.

DRY ROASTED PEANUTS

3 cups raw peanuts, shelled
2 tablespoons butter or oleo, melted
Salt

Preheat oven to 350°. Spread peanuts in 15x10x1 inch baking pan. Roast for 35 minutes. Stir often. Check on brownness occasionally by removing skins from a few nuts. Cool peanuts, slip off skins. Stir salt into butter. Coat peanuts well. Dry on paper towels.

FROSTED FILBERTS

1 egg white
2 tablespoons cold water
½ teaspoon salt
½ teaspoon cinnamon
¼ teaspoon cloves
¼ teaspoon allspice
½ cup sugar
2 cups filberts

Beat egg white with water, salt, and spices til soft peaks form. Gradually add sugar til very stiff peaks form. Add a few filberts, stir to coat. Place one at a time on greased cookie sheet. Bake at 275° for 40 minutes. Cool. Store in tins.

GLAZED ALMONDS

2 cups blanched almonds
1 cup sugar
½ cup water

Put all ingredients in saucepan on high heat and cook til all water is gone. Lower heat and stir rapidly til white look disappears from almonds and nuts are coated with brown syrup. Pour onto buttered cookie sheet and let cool. Break apart. Store in tins.

GLAZED PECANS

2 cups pecan halves
½ cup butter or oleo
¼ cup light corn syrup
Salt

Spread pecans in roasting pan, dot with butter and drizzle with syrup. Roast at 250° for 1 hour, stirring often. Spread on wax paper. Salt generously.

HERBED PECANS

3 tablespoons butter or oleo
3 tablespoons Worcestershire
1 teaspoon salt
½ teaspoon cinnamon
¼ teaspoon garlic powder
¼ teaspoon cayenne
Dash Tabasco sauce
2 cups pecans

In saucepan, combine butter, Worcestershire, salt, cinnamon, garlic powder, cayenne and Tabasco sauce. Stir til blended. Add pecans, toss til coated. Place in single layer in roasting pan, bake at 300° for 25 minutes, stirring often. Drain on paper towels. Store in tins.

ORANGE PECANS

3 cups pecan halves
1 tablespoon orange peel
½ cup orange juice
1½ cups sugar

Combine sugar, juice, and peel. Cook to 236° on candy thermometer. Add pecans, stir with wooden spoon til opaque. Drop on wax paper. Separate pecans. Store in tins.

PEPPERED PECANS

4 cups pecan halves
2 tablespoons butter or oleo
2 teaspoons Worcestershire
3 dashes Tabasco
Salt, white pepper to taste

Saute pecans in butter. Add remaining ingredients. Toast at 300° 20 minutes.

PEPPY NUTS

2 tablespoons butter or oleo
1 teaspoon salt
1 teaspoon celery salt
1 teaspoon chili powder
⅛ teaspoon cayenne
1½ cups nuts

In roasting pan, combine butter, salt, celery salt, chili powder and cayenne. Stir in nuts. Bake at 375° for 15 minutes, stirring often. Drain on paper towels. Store in tins. Especially good with whole almonds.

SHERRIED WALNUTS

1½ cups brown sugar
¼ cup sherry
2 tablespoons corn syrup
1 teaspoon pumpkin pie spice
¼ teaspoon salt
5 cups walnut halves
Granulated sugar

In saucepan, heat brown sugar, sherry, corn syrup, pumpkin pie spice and salt til sugar is dissolved. Stir in walnuts, coat well. Roll in granulated sugar. Dry on baking sheet.

SOUR CREAM SUGARED NUTS

½ cup sour cream
1½ cups sugar
1½ teaspoons vanilla
3 cups walnuts

Heat cream and sugar to 223° on candy thermometer, stirring constantly. Add vanilla and nuts. Stir rapidly til mixture coats nuts and sugars. Spread on tray, separate nuts. Cool thoroughly. Store in airtight tins. Will keep several months.

SPICED NUTS

1 cup sugar
1 teaspoon salt
4 tablespoons water
½ teaspoon cinnamon
2 cups toasted pecan halves

Cook sugar, salt, water and cinnamon to 242° on candy thermometer. Remove from heat, add pecan halves, toss to coat pecans. Pour on cookie sheet, separate, and cool. Store in tins.

SUGARED NUTS

1 cup brown sugar
2 cups maple syrup
6 cups pecans
Granulated sugar
Powdered sugar

In saucepan, boil brown sugar and maple syrup to 230° on candy thermometer. Cool slightly. In pan, coat nuts, repeating til all nuts are covered. Dust with powdered sugar. Dry in cool place before storing in tins. Any other blanched nuts may be used.

SWEDISH NUTS

4 cups pecans, English walnuts, almonds, or combination, halved
1 cup sugar
Dash salt
2 egg whites, stiffly beaten
½ cup butter or oleo

Preheat oven to 325°. Toast nuts in oven til light brown. Fold sugar and salt into egg whites. Beat til stiff peaks form. Fold nuts into meringue. Melt butter in 15½x10½x1 inch jelly roll pan. Spread nut mixture over butter. Bake 30 minutes, stirring every 10 minutes. Cool.

PECAN SNACK

Put 2 pecan halves together with anchovy paste or cream cheese mixed with anchovy paste.

APPETIZERS

COCKTAIL MIX

1 pound box Wheat Chex
1 box Cheerios
1 pound butter or oleo
4 cups raw mixed nuts or raw pecans
1 box pretzel sticks
1 tablespoon celery salt
1 tablespoon salt
1 tablespoon garlic salt

Mix ingredients in large roasting pan. Dot with butter. Cook uncovered in 250° oven for 2 hours, stirring well every half hour. Store in air-tight containers. Mixture will keep indefinitely.

CHICKEN SUPREME DIP

1 8 ounce cream cheese
1 small can mushroom pieces
½ cup almonds, chopped
1 can boned chicken
Dash garlic salt
Dash Worcestershire

Melt cream cheese and add mushroom pieces, almonds, chicken, garlic salt and Worcestershire. Serve warm in chafing dish with chips or melba rounds.

HOT TUNA DIP

1 8 ounce cream cheese
1 9¼ ounce can tuna
1 can cream of mushroom soup
1 small can mushrooms
Garlic powder, Worcestershire to taste
¼ cup almonds, chopped

Heat cream cheese and soup til well blended. Add other ingredients. Serve warm in chafing dish with chips.

ALMOND CHEESE BALL

1 3 ounce cream cheese
½ pound Cheddar cheese, grated
¼ cup pimiento, chopped
¾ cup almonds, sliced
1 tablespoon lemon juice
½ teaspoon salt
1 teaspoon Worcestershire
1 teaspoon onion, grated
Dash cayenne
¼ cup almonds, chopped

Soften cheeses, mix all ingredients together except chopped almonds and shape into ball. Roll in last ¼ cup almonds. Chill.

CHEESE ROLL

1 8 ounce cream cheese
1 glass Old English cheese
½ pound Cheddar cheese, grated
2 cloves garlic, crushed
Few drops each, Tabasco and Worcestershire
Chili powder
Paprika
1 cup pecans or walnuts, chopped

Soften cheeses, mix together with garlic, Tabasco and Worcestershire. Sprinkle wax paper with chili powder and paprika. Roll cheese in wax paper, chill. Roll in nuts.

CHILI CHEESE BALL

1 8 ounce cream cheese
½ pound Cheddar cheese, grated
2 cloves garlic, minced
1 cup pecans, chopped
2 tablespoons chili powder

Soften cheeses, blend in garlic. Mix in pecans, shape into ball. Roll in chili powder. Chill. Serve with crackers.

PINEAPPLE CHEESE BALL

2 8 ounce cream cheese
1 small can crushed pineapple, drained
¼ cup bell pepper, chopped
2 tablespoons onion, chopped
1 tablespoon salt
1 cup pecans, chopped

Mix all ingredients except pecans. Shape into ball. Roll in pecans. Chill.

SUPER SALMON LOG

1 1 pound can salmon, skinned and boned
1 8 ounce cream cheese
1 tablespoon lemon juice
2 teaspoons grated onion
1 teaspoon horseradish
¼ teaspoon salt
½ cup pecans, chopped
3 tablespoons parsley

Flake salmon, combine with cream cheese, lemon juice, grated onion, horseradish and salt. Chill. Shape into log and roll in parsley and nuts.

TURKEY BALL

1 cup cooked turkey, ground
3 tablespoons bacon-flavored bits
¼ cup creamy Roquefort salad dressing
¼ cup pecans, chopped

Combine turkey, bacon bits and salad dressing. Chill. Form into ball. Roll in nuts. Serve with crackers.

TURKEY CHEESE BALL

1 8 ounce cream cheese
1 cup cooked turkey, ground
¾ cup toasted almonds, chopped
⅓ cup mayonnaise
2 tablespoons chutney
1 tablespoon curry powder
¼ teaspoon salt
Chopped parsley

Mix together all ingredients except parsley. Chill. Form into ball. Roll in parsley. Serve with crackers.

CAMENBERT PISTACHIO

1 8 ounce whole ripe Camenbert
1 cup dry white wine
1 stick butter or oleo
½ cup pistachios, chopped
½ cup pistachios, ground

If very ripe, scrape Camenbert lightly. Place in bowl, cover with wine, let stand 24 hours. Drain off wine and reserve. Add butter with cheese and mash to smooth paste. Add one or two teaspoonfuls of wine to cheese, but do not make runny. Add the nuts. Chill mixture. Shape into round like original cheese. Roll in ground nuts. Chill. Set out 30 minutes before serving. Serve with unsalted crackers, French bread, and additional butter.

APPETIZER PIE

1 8 ounce cream cheese
2 tablespoons milk
1 2½ ounce jar sliced dried beef, chopped
2 tablespoons minced onion
2 tablespoons green pepper, chopped
⅛ teaspoon pepper
½ cup sour cream
¼ cup walnuts, chopped

Soften cream cheese, blend with milk. Stir in dried beef, onion, green pepper and pepper, mix well. Stir in sour cream. Spoon into 8 inch pie plate. Sprinkle with walnuts. Bake at 350° for 15 minutes. Serve hot with crackers.

BACON-CHEESE SPREAD

1 pound extra sharp Cheddar cheese, grated
16 slices crisp bacon, crumbled
1 teaspoon salt
12 green onions, chopped (tops, too)
1 cup toasted almonds, slivered
2 cups mayonnaise

Mix all ingredients together. Serve on crackers or melba rounds.

CHIPPED BEEF SPREAD

- 2 8 ounce cream cheese
- 4 tablespoons milk
- 6 ounces chipped beef, chopped
- 1 cup sour cream
- ½ cup green pepper, chopped
- 2 tablespoons onion flakes
- ½ teaspoon pepper
- ½ teaspoon garlic salt
- 1 cup chopped pecans, sauteed in 4 tablespoons butter

Soften cream cheese and mix with all ingredients except pecans. Put in small baking dish, top with pecans and bake at 350° for 20 minutes. Serve with crackers.

CURRY NUT SPREAD

- 2 8 ounce cream cheese, softened
- ½ cup chopped chutney
- 2 teaspoons curry powder
- ½ teaspoon dry mustard
- ½ cup toasted almonds, chopped

With hands mix cream cheese with rest of ingredients. Shape into ball. Refrigerate. Remove from refrigerator 20 minutes before serving. Sprinkle generously with paprika. Serve with crackers. Keeps in refrigerator for 1 month.

DEVILED PEANUT SPREAD

- ½ cup peanut butter
- 1 2¼ ounce can deviled ham
- ½ teaspoon celery salt

Mix all ingredients. Serve on crackers.

LIVER PATÉ WITH WALNUTS

- 1 envelope unflavored gelatin
- 1 can consommé Madrilene
- 2 hard boiled eggs, chopped
- 2 4¾ ounce liver spread
- ½ cup walnuts, chopped
- 1 tablespoon sweet pickle relish, drained
- ½ teaspoon salt
- ¼ teaspoon pepper

In saucepan, mix gelatin with Madrilene, let stand 1 minute. Stir over medium heat til gelatin completely dissolves. In 3 cup bowl pour layer of gelatin mixture about ½ inch deep. Refrigerate until almost firm, about 15 minutes. Cool remaining gelatin at room temperature. Force eggs through sieve over remaining gelatin mixture. Add remaining ingredients and beat til well blended. Pour over gelatin layer in bowl. Chill until firm, 4 hours or overnight. Unmold onto serving plate and serve with crackers.

RICH MAN POOR MAN SPECIAL

1½ pound sharp Cheddar cheese, grated
1 envelope unflavored gelatin
1 cup pecans, chopped
1 small can ripe olives, chopped
1 teaspoon cayenne pepper
1 cup Worcestershire sauce
¾ cup hot water

Soak gelatin in 2 tablespoons cold water. Combine cheese, Worcestershire, hot water and gelatin. Blend til smooth. Add rest of ingredients. Pour into 1 quart mold. Refrigerate overnight. Unmold on plate, garnish with stuffed green olives. Serve with crackers.

BLENDER BUTTER

2 tablespoons salad oil
1½ cups salted filberts, pecans, English or black walnuts, or almonds

Put vegetable oil in blender, add nuts, cover and process on blend til desired consistency. If necessary stop and push down with rubber spatula, cover and continue blending. If unsalted nuts are used, add salt to taste for flavor.

BLENDER PEANUT BUTTER

Put 1½ cups salted peanuts into blender, cover and process at blend until of desired consistency. If unsalted peanuts are used add ½ teaspoon salt for each cup of nuts. If necessary stop and push down with rubber spatula, cover and continue processing.

ENERGY BUTTER

½ cup unroasted cashews
¼ cup sesame seeds
¼ cup sunflower seeds, shelled
3 tablespoons corn oil
¼ teaspoon salt
⅓ cup raisins, chopped

In blender combine cashews, sesame seeds and sunflower seeds. Cover, blend on low speed til finely chopped, then on medium high speed til pureed smooth. Stop often and scrape puree from sides of blender. Add oil and salt, blend til smooth. Stir in raisins.

APPETIZERS

ALMOND PASTE

1 pound almonds, ground
1 box powdered sugar
2 egg whites, unbeaten
2 teaspoons almond extract

Combine egg whites with sugar, add flavoring, cream well. Add almonds.

STUFFED CELERY

1 3 ounce cream cheese
1 tablespoon parsley
½ teaspoon minced onion
2 tablespoons nuts, chopped

Blend together cream cheese, parsley and minced onion. Fill five celery stalks. Sprinkle with chopped nuts.

CHEESE STUFFED CELERY

1 3 ounce cream cheese, softened
2 tablespoons mustard
1 8 ounce jar sharp cheese
1 cup pecans, finely chopped
2 tablespoons Worcestershire
Celery
Paprika

Combine cream cheese, mustard, sharp cheese, nuts, and Worcestershire, blend well by hand. Stuff celery cut into 2 inch lengths. Sprinkle with paprika.

PARTY MUSHROOMS

24 large fresh mushrooms
¼ cup butter or oleo
1 envelope onion soup mix
¾ cup dry bread crumbs
½ cup almonds, chopped
⅓ cup sherry
2 tablespoons butter or oleo
¼ cup Parmesan cheese, grated

Remove stems from mushrooms, chop stems and set aside. In skillet, melt butter, add stems, and cook until tender. Add onion soup mix, bread crumbs and almonds, mix well. Stir in sherry. Fill caps with mixture. Place in pan, brush with butter, sprinkle with cheese, broil 5 minutes. Serve with toothpicks or on toast points.

CHEESE CRISPIES

- ½ pound sharp Cheddar cheese, grated
- 1 stick butter or oleo
- 1 tablespoon Worcestershire
- 1¼ cups flour
- ½ teaspoon salt
- Dash red pepper
- Dash Tabasco
- 1 cup pecans, chopped

Cream together butter and cheese, add remaining ingredients. Chill. Roll into 2 long logs 1 inch wide. Store in refrigerator indefinitely. Take out and let stand 5 minutes. Slice into thin rounds. Bake at 350° for 10 minutes on ungreased cookie sheets.

CORN NUT CRUMBLES

- 1 8½ ounce package corn muffin mix
- 1 cup salted peanuts, chopped
- ½ cup grated Parmesan cheese
- 1 teaspoon garlic powder
- 3 tablespoons butter or oleo, melted

Preheat oven to 375°. Prepare corn mix according to package directions. Spread batter in greased 15½x10½x1 inch baking pan. Sprinkle with nuts, cheese and garlic powder. Drizzle with butter. Bake 20 to 25 minutes. Immediately cut into squares, cool slightly. Makes 48.

OLIVE NUT SLICES

- 1½ cups flour
- ¾ teaspoon salt
- ½ teaspoon paprika
- ½ cup butter or oleo
- ½ cup sour cream
- ¾ cup pecans, chopped
- ¾ cup Cheddar cheese, grated
- ¾ cup pimiento-stuffed green olives, chopped
- 2 tablespoons mayonnaise

Preheat oven to 400°. Sift flour with salt and paprika. Cut in butter. Add sour cream, mix well. Cover and chill ½ hour. Mix together rest of ingredients. Divide dough into 2 balls. Roll each into a 8x14 inch rectangle. Cut each into 2 4 inch wide strips. Spread olive filling down center of each strip. Fold long sides together, pinch to seal. Pinch ends together. Place on cookie sheet, seam side down. Bake for 20 minutes. Cool. Slice. Makes 36.

CHEESE BISCUITS

- 1 small jar cheese spread
- 1 stick butter or oleo
- 1¼ cups flour
- 2 tablespoons nuts, chopped
- Red Pepper

Bring cheese and butter to room temperature, add other ingredients. Form into small balls, press flat with fork. Bake on greased cookie sheet at 325° for 10 to 20 minutes.

MACADAMIA BISCUITS

- ¼ cup butter or oleo
- 1 cup biscuit mix
- 1 egg, slightly beaten
- 1 cup Macadamia nuts, chopped
- ½ cup Cheddar cheese, grated
- Red Pepper

Preheat oven to 400°. Cut butter into biscuit mix. Stir in remaining ingredients. Drop by teaspoonful onto greased cookie sheet. Bake for 8 minutes.

ANCHOVY PECAN PUFFS

- ½ cup butter or oleo
- 1 3 ounce cream cheese
- 1 cup flour
- 1 tube anchovy paste
- ½ cup pecans, chopped

Soften butter and cheese, blend well. Add flour and chill. Roll very thin and cut with small biscuit cutter. Spread with anchovy paste and sprinkle a few pecans on top. Fold over to make puff. Bake at 400° for 10 minutes. Serve hot. Easy and delicious. Makes 45.

PARTY PUFFS

- 1 cup cooked chicken, chopped
- ½ cup celery, chopped
- ¼ cup almonds, chopped
- Mayonnaise
- Salt, pepper, lemon juice to taste

Combine ingredients for chicken salad. Refrigerate.

Puff Shells:

- ½ cup boiling water
- ¼ cup butter or oleo
- ½ cup flour
- 2 unbeaten eggs

In saucepan, melt butter in water. Add flour all at once and stir vigorously. When ball forms in center of pan, remove from heat and cool 5 minutes. Add 1 egg and beat thoroughly. Add 2nd egg and beat again. Drop 1 teaspoon at a time 2 inches apart on greased cookie sheet. Bake at 375° til all moisture beads disappear, about 25 minutes. When cool, fill with chicken salad. Puffs can be made ahead and frozen, then filled the day you use them. Keep refrigerated until serving.

CHICKEN NUT PUFFS

1 cup chicken broth
½ cup butter or oleo
2 teaspoons seasoned salt
2 teaspoons Worcestershire
¾ teaspoon celery seed
⅛ teaspoon cayenne
1 cup flour
1 tablespoon parsley
½ teaspoon paprika
1 5 ounce can boneless chicken
4 eggs
½ cup toasted almonds, chopped

In saucepan, combine chicken broth and butter, bring to boil. Stir in salt, Worcestershire, celery seed, cayenne, flour, parsley, and paprika. Cook until mixture leaves sides of pan and forms ball. Remove from heat, add eggs one at a time, beating well after each, until mixture is shiny. Stir in chicken and almonds. Drop by teaspoonful onto ungreased cookie sheet. Bake at 400° for 15-18 minutes. Serve hot. Makes 75.

CHICKEN TEA SANDWICHES

2 3 ounce cream cheese
2 4¾ ounce cans chicken spread
4 teaspoons candied ginger, chopped
¼ cup almonds, slivered

Soften cream cheese, blend all ingredients. Chill. Spread onto crusted bread. Cut into finger sandwiches.

OLIVE NUT SANDWICHES

3 3 ounce cream cheese
1 small can ripe olives, chopped
1 small onion, grated
1 cup nuts, chopped
Salt and pepper to taste
Dash red pepper
1 teaspoon lemon juice
½ cup mayonnaise

Mix ingredients in order given. Spread on crusted bread, cut into finger sandwiches. Also good as dip or spread for crackers.

ROLLED SANDWICHES

1 8 ounce cream cheese
1 can mushroom soup
1 small can mushroom pieces
½ cup almonds, chopped
Pinch garlic powder
½ tablespoon Worcestershire
½ tablespoon horseradish

Mix in order given. Remove crusts from bread. Put teaspoonful on one slice bread. Roll. Fasten with toothpicks. Refrigerate overnight. Brush with melted butter. Toast at 450°. Great do-ahead dish!

SANDWICH DELITE

1 loaf thin sliced bread
1 8 ounce cream cheese
1 small jar apple jelly
1 stick butter or oleo
1 cup pecans, chopped

Make a 3 decker sandwich as follows:
1st slice—spread with pecans and cream cheese.
2nd slice—thinly spread butter and apple jelly. Put 3rd slice on top. Trim outside crust. Cut sandwich in half.

TUNA MUFFIN

1 cup creamed cottage cheese
1 7 ounce can tuna
½ cup mayonnaise
¼ cup celery, chopped
¼ cup green onion, chopped
5 radishes, diced
Salt and pepper to taste
½ cup toasted almonds, slivered
6 English muffins, split and toasted

Combine all ingredients. Spread on six muffin halves. Top with remaining halves.

TUNA SURPRISE

1 7 ounce can tuna
1 cup unpared apple, chopped
¼ cup walnuts, chopped
½ cup mayonnaise
1 3½ ounce can fried onions
12 slices white bread, buttered
6 slices American cheese
6 slices whole wheat bread, buttered

Combine apple, nuts, tuna and mayonnaise, set aside. Arrange onions atop six slices of white bread. Cover onion with slice of cheese, top with slice whole wheat bread. Spread whole wheat slice with tuna mixture, top with remaining slices of bread. Makes six sandwiches. Cut each sandwich into fourths to serve.

TURKEY BURGERS

2 cups cooked turkey, chopped
1 egg, slightly beaten
½ cup mayonnaise
¼ cup bread crumbs
2 tablespoons onion, chopped
2 tablespoons nuts, chopped
¼ teaspoon salt
1 tablespoon butter or oleo
Bread crumbs
3 English muffins, split and toasted
Lettuce

Mix together turkey, egg, mayonnaise, bread crumbs, onion, nuts and salt. Chill. Shape into six patties, roll in bread crumbs. Melt butter, cook patties 10 minutes over medium heat. Serve on muffin halves with lettuce.

HOMEMADE GRANOLA

2½ cups old fashioned rolled oats
1 cup coconut, shredded
½ cup almonds, chopped
½ cup sesame seeds
½ cup sunflower seeds, shelled
½ cup unsweetened wheat germ
½ cup honey
¼ cup cooking oil
½ cup dried apricots, chopped
½ cup raisins

Preheat oven to 300°. In large bowl combine oats, coconut, almonds, sesame seeds, sunflower seeds, and wheat germ. Combine honey and oil. Stir into oat mixture. Spread out in 13x9x2 inch baking pan. Bake about 45 or 50 minutes, stirring every 15 minutes. Remove from oven, stir in dried apricots and raisins. Pour into another pan to cool. Stir occasionally. Store in tightly covered jars or plastic bags. If keeping more than 2 weeks, freeze.

Salads

Salads

QUICKIE

Peel banana, leave whole. Roll in mayonnaise, roll in chopped pecans. Serve on lettuce or as dessert.

BEET SALAD

Serves 8

1 20 ounce can crushed pineapple
1 16 ounce can julienne beets
½ cup water
¼ cup vinegar
2 tablespoons sugar
3 tablespoons lemon juice
2 3 ounce packages black raspberry Jello
½ cup nuts, chopped

Drain pineapple and beets, reserving liquid. Combine liquid and water, vinegar, sugar and lemon juice, bring to boil. Dissolve Jello in hot liquid. Chill until consistency of unbeaten egg whites. Stir in pineapple, nuts, and beets. Pour into mold. Chill until firm.

ALMOND BROCCOLI SALAD

1 bunch fresh broccoli
1 bottle vinaigrette dressing
1 hard-cooked egg, chopped
1 tablespoon minced parsley
⅓ cup almonds, chopped

Wash broccoli and cook in boiling water 15 minutes. Drain, pour vinaigrette dressing over, chill thoroughly. Serve on lettuce leaves with remaining ingredients sprinkled on top.

CARROT SALAD

Serves 4

1 3 ounce package orange Jello
2 cups boiling water
2 cups carrots, grated
½ cup coconut, grated
1 8¼ ounce can crushed pineapple, drained
¼ cup pecans, chopped

Dissolve Jello in boiling water. Chill until mixture is consistency of unbeaten egg whites. Stir in other ingredients, pour into mold. Chill.

KIDNEY BEAN SALAD

6 hard boiled eggs
1 20 ounce can red kidney beans, drained
1 cup nuts, chopped
½ cup ripe olives, sliced
1 green onion, minced
⅓ cup mayonnaise
2 tablespoons milk
1 teaspoon prepared mustard
Salt and pepper

Remove 1 egg yolk from white, crumble yolk and set aside. Cut remaining eggs in chunks, toss lightly with beans, nuts, olives, and onion. Chill at least ½ hour. Blend mayonnaise, milk, and mustard, spoon over egg-bean mixture, toss lightly. Season. Line salad bowl with lettuce, fill with salad, sprinkle with crumbled egg yolk.

WATERCRESS SALAD

1 large bunch watercress, torn
½ cup fresh mushrooms, sliced
½ cup canned hearts of palms, sliced
¼ cup toasted almonds, chopped
Salt and pepper
¼ cup creamy garlic salad dressing

Toss ingredients together except salad dressing. Add water to salad dressing to make ⅓ cup. Mix well, pour over salad. Toss gently.

FRUITED COLESLAW

1 large head cabbage, shredded
1 8 ounce can crushed pineapple, drained
1 cup toasted almonds
1 cup Cool Whip
1 cup mayonnaise
Salt and pepper

Combine all ingredients, toss well. Chill at least 1 hour before serving.

PEANUT-BANANA COLESLAW

2 bananas, sliced
2 tablespoons lemon juice
4 cups cabbage, finely shredded
½ cup mayonnaise
Salt and pepper to taste
¼ cup salted peanuts, chopped

Toss bananas and lemon juice. Add cabbage, mayonnaise, salt and pepper. Spoon into serving dish, chill. Before serving sprinkle with peanuts. Serves 6.

BANANA LAYER SALAD

5 large bananas, sliced
1 package miniature marshmallows
3 tablespoons sugar
1 tablespoon mayonnaise
1 pint cream, whipped
1 cup peanuts, chopped finely
Red pepper

In oblong dish place layer of bananas and layer of marshmallows. Fold sugar and mayonnaise into cream. Top bananas with mixture. Sprinkle with peanuts and red pepper. Repeat layers until all ingredients are used. Serves 6.

BLACK WALNUT-PERSIMMON SALAD

1 11 ounce can mandarin oranges
2 cups apples, diced
2 bananas, sliced
½ cup persimmon, peeled and sliced
¼ cup black walnuts, chopped
½ cup mayonnaise
¼ cup Cool Whip
1 teaspoon sugar

Serves 6
Drain oranges, combine fruits and nuts, stirring gently. Combine remaining ingredients, mix well, pour over fruit mixture. Toss gently. Chill 2 hours.

MILLIONAIRE SALAD

1 large can pineapple chunks, drained and reserve liquid
1 large can Queen Anne cherries, seeded
1 16 ounce bag marshmallows, cut
3 cups almonds, slivered
1 pint whipping cream, whipped

Fruit Dressing:
5 tablespoons lemon juice
2 tablespoons sugar
3 egg yolks
1 heaping tablespoon cornstarch
1½ teaspoon salt
Juice from pineapple chunks

Serves 12
Cook dressing in double boiler until very thick. Drain fruit, add marshmallows, nuts, and dressing. Fold in whipped cream. Make this salad the day before needed. Refrigerate or freeze. Stir once or twice.

RED HOT APPLE SALAD

Serves 6

½ cup red cinnamon candies
2 cups water
6 small tart apples, pared and cored
1 3 ounce cream cheese, softened
2 tablespoons milk
1 teaspoon lemon juice
1 8¾ ounce can crushed pineapple, drained
½ cup dates, chopped
2 tablespoons chopped nuts
Lettuce

In saucepan cook cinnamon candies in water til dissolved. Add apples, cook slowly til tender, 15 to 20 minutes, stirring once. Refrigerate apples in syrup several hours, turning once. Blend together cream cheese, milk, lemon juice til creamy. Add pineapple, dates and nuts. Drain apples. Fill centers with cream cheese mixture. Serve on lettuce.

SIX CUP SALAD

Serves 8-10

1 cup miniature marshmallows
1 cup mandarin oranges, drained
1 cup pineapple chunks, drained
1 cup sour cream
1 cup coconut, grated
1 cup pecans, chopped

Combine all ingredients and refrigerate at least one hour or overnight.

APRICOT SALAD

Serves 6-8

1 small package lemon or apricot Jello
1 large can peeled apricots, drained
2 tablespoons lemon juice
⅓ cup orange juice
1 cup slivered almonds or chopped pecans
1 3 ounce cream cheese
½ cup Ginger Ale

Purée apricots. Dissolve Jello in hot purée. Add juices and nuts. Put small ball of cream cheese in center of individual molds. Pour in Jello mixture. Refrigerate. Serve with mayonnaise.

NUTTY CARROT PINEAPPLE SALAD

1 cup boiling water
1 3 ounce package lemon Jello
1 cup pineapple juice
1 tablespoon lemon juice
½ teaspoon salt
1 cup crushed pineapple
1 cup carrots, grated
½ cup walnuts, chopped

Serves 6-8

Stir Jello in boiling water til dissolved. Add juices and salt. Chill til slightly thickened. Add pineapple, carrots and nuts. Pour into individual molds or 5 cup mold. Refrigerate.

AVOCADO-CRANBERRY SALAD

2 3 ounce packages raspberry Jello
½ cup sugar
2 cups boiling water
1½ cups cold water
1 cup fresh cranberries, ground
Dash salt
1 avocado, peeled and cubed
¼ cup nuts, chopped

Serves 8

Dissolve Jello and sugar in boiling water, add cold water. Chill til slightly thickened. Combine remaining ingredients. Pour into mold. Chill til firm.

BLUE DEVIL SALAD

1 6 ounce package raspberry Jello
1 cup boiling water
1 21 ounce can blueberry pie filling
1 8¼ ounce can crushed pineapple, drained
1 8 ounce cream cheese, softened
1 cup sour cream
1 cup nuts
½ cup sugar

Serves 8-10

Dissolve Jello in 2 quart dish. Add pie filling and pineapple. Chill until firm. Combine cream cheese, sour cream, nuts and sugar. Spread over congealed mixture. Chill.

CALIFORNIA AVOCADO SALAD

Serves 6-8

1 3 ounce package lime Jello
1 cup hot water
1 large can crushed pineapple, (drain and reserve juice)
1 cup ripe avocado, chopped
½ cup walnuts, chopped
2 tablespoons lemon juice
½ cup mayonnaise
½ cup Cool Whip
¼ teaspoon salt

Dissolve gelatin in hot water and cool. Add pineapple juice, lemon juice, mayonnaise, and salt. Beat well with mixer, chill til thickened. Put in freezer in ice trays for 15 minutes. Pour into mixing bowl, beat til fluffy. Fold in Cool Whip, avocado, nuts and pineapple. Pour into mold and refrigerate.

CHERRIES JUBILEE SALAD

Serves 8

1 16 ounce can pitted dark sweet cherries, halved
1 3 ounce package cherry Jello
½ cup cream sherry
1 16 ounce can pear halves, drained
1 3 ounce cream cheese, cut into small cubes
¼ cup pecans, chopped
Lettuce leaves

Drain cherries, reserve liquid. Add water to liquid to make 1½ cups. In saucepan combine Jello and syrup mixture. Heat and stir til gelatin dissolves. Remove from heat, stir in sherry. Chill til partially set. Chop all but 2 pear halves, fold into gelatin along with cherries, cheese, and pecans. Pour into 4½ cup molds. Chill until firm. Unmold, garnish with lettuce leaves and reserved pears, sliced.

CRANBERRY ORANGE MOLD

Serves 8

2 oranges
2 3 ounce packages strawberry Jello
¼ teaspoon salt
1½ cups boiling water
1 16 ounce can jellied cranberry sauce
⅔ cup nuts, chopped

Grate 1 tablespoon orange rind. Section oranges, dice sections, and drain. Dissolve Jello and salt in boiling water. Stir cranberry sauce til smooth, blend into Jello with orange rind. Chill til slightly thickened. Fold in diced oranges and nuts. Pour into mold. Chill until firm.

HOLIDAY CRANBERRY SALAD

- 1 3 ounce package strawberry Jello
- 1 3 ounce package raspberry Jello
- 3 cups boiling water
- 1 cup pineapple juice
- 1 pound cranberries, ground
- 1 small apple, grated
- 1 15¼ ounce can crushed pineapple, drained
- 1 cup sugar
- 1 cup nuts, chopped
- 12 marshmallows, cut in fourths

Serves 8-10

Dissolve Jello in boiling water, add pineapple juice, cool. Combine remaining ingredients, add to gelatin. Pour into oblong pan, chill until firm. Serve in squares.

PEAR-GRAPE RING

- 1 envelope unflavored gelatin
- ½ cup cold water
- ¼ cup sugar
- ½ teaspoon salt
- 1 tablespoon lemon juice
- 1 cup Ginger Ale
- 1 medium pear, peeled and diced
- ⅔ cup red grapes, halved and seeded
- ¼ cup nuts, chopped

Serves 4

Let gelatin soak in cold water 1 minute. Cook and stir over low heat until dissolved. Remove from heat, stir in sugar, salt and lemon juice til sugar dissolves. Stir in Ginger Ale. Chill until thickened. Fold in pear, grapes and nuts. Pour into small ring mold and chill until firm.

SUMMER CANTALOUPE SALAD

- 1 3 ounce package lemon Jello
- ⅛ teaspoon salt
- 1 cup hot water
- 1 cup cold water
- 1 teaspoon lemon juice
- 1 cup cantaloupe balls
- ¼ cup celery, chopped
- ¼ cup nuts, chopped
- 1 3 ounce cream cheese, softened
- 2 tablespoons mayonnaise

Serves 6-8

Dissolve Jello and salt in hot water, add cold water and lemon juice. Chill ½ mixture til slightly thickened. Fold in cantaloupe, celery and nuts, pour into 1 quart mold and chill until almost firm. Blend together cheese and mayonnaise. Gradually add remaining Jello. Pour over chilled mixture. Chill until firm.

FRUIT SALAD DRESSING

2 3 ounce cream cheese
1 cup mayonnaise
1 cup whipped cream
1½ cups nuts, chopped

Soften cream cheese and blend with mayonnaise. Fold in whipped cream and nuts. Serve over fruit salads.

EFIRD'S FROZEN FRUIT SALAD

2 3 ounce cream cheese, softened
⅓ cup mayonnaise
Dash salt
½ cup whipped cream
3½ cups fruit cocktail, drained
½ cup chopped nuts

Blend cream cheese, mayonnaise and salt. Fold in whipped cream. Fold in fruit cocktail and nuts. Spoon into baking pan. Freeze for several hours or overnight. Cut into squares to serve.

FROZEN AVOCADO SALAD

1 8 ounce cream cheese, softened
1 cup sour cream
¼ teaspoon salt
½ cup sugar
1 avocado, diced
1 grapefruit, sectioned
1 cup white grapes
½ cup pecans, chopped

Blend cream cheese and sour cream, add salt and sugar. Stir til smooth. Add remaining ingredients. Freeze in cupcake papers in muffin tins or in 9x5 inch pan. Serves 8.

FROZEN FRUIT SALAD

Serves 12

1 can Eagle Brand milk
¼ cup lemon juice
1 medium can crushed pineapple
1 21 ounce can cherry pie filling
1 cup pecans, chopped
1 10 ounce Cool Whip

Mix all ingredients until well blended. Fill paper cup cake liners in muffin tins and freeze. When frozen, remove from pans and put in plastic bags. Seal and keep in freezer until needed.

FROZEN PINK SALAD

Serves 8-10

- 2 3 ounce cream cheese, softened
- 2 tablespoons mayonnaise
- 2 tablespoons sugar
- 1 16 ounce can whole cranberry sauce
- 1 8¼ ounce can crushed pineapple, drained
- ½ cup nuts, chopped
- 1 cup whipping cream, whipped

Combine cream cheese, mayonnaise, and sugar, blend until smooth. Add cranberry sauce, pineapple, and nuts, mix well. Fold in whipped cream. Pour into loaf pan and freeze. To serve let stand at room temperature 15 minutes, slice.

FROZEN WALDORF SALAD

Serves 8

- 1 medium can crushed pineapple
- 2 eggs, slightly beaten
- ½ cup sugar
- ¼ cup lemon juice
- ⅛ teaspoon salt
- ½ cup whipping cream, whipped
- 2½ cups unpeeled apple, diced
- ½ cup celery, chopped
- ½ cup nuts, chopped

Drain pineapple, reserving juice. Combine juice with eggs, sugar, lemon juice, and salt. Cook over low heat, stirring constantly, until slightly thickened. Cool. Fold remaining ingredients into cooked mixture. Spoon into 8 inch square pan, freeze. Serve in squares.

ARKANSAS CHICKEN RICE SALAD

Serves 6

- 1 tablespoon lemon juice
- ¾ cup mayonnaise
- 2 cups cooked white rice
- 2 cups cooked chicken, diced
- 1 cup celery, chopped
- ½ cup pimiento stuffed green olives, sliced
- ¼ cup toasted almonds, sliced
- 2 tablespoons green onions, thinly sliced
- 6 lettuce cups

Add lemon juice to mayonnaise, blend well. Combine remaining ingredients except lettuce. Mix lightly, chill. Serve in individual lettuce cups.

TURKEY WALDORF SALAD

Serves 5-6

- 1 medium apple, cored and diced
- 1 tablespoon lemon juice
- 2 cups cooked turkey, diced
- 1 cup red grapes, halved and seeded
- 1 cup celery, chopped
- 1/4 cup walnuts, chopped
- 1/4 cup onion, chopped
- 2/3 cup mayonnaise
- 1/2 teaspoon salt
- Dash pepper
- Lettuce
- 1 hard boiled egg

Chill ingredients. Sprinkle diced apple with lemon juice. Add turkey, grapes, celery, nuts, onions, mayonnaise, salt and pepper and toss lightly. Serve in lettuce lined bowl. Cut white of egg into wedges, arrange on top in shape of flowers. Top with grated yolk.

CRANBERRY-FILBERT RELISH

- 1 20 ounce can crushed pineapple
- 2 cups sugar
- 4 cups cranberries
- 2 oranges
- 1/2 cup seedless raisins
- 1/2 cup candied ginger, chopped
- 1/2 cup toasted filberts, chopped

Drain pineapple, measure syrup, add enough water to make 2 cups. Add sugar to liquid, bring to boil, stirring until sugar is dissolved. Add cranberries, cook 5 minutes. Grate rind of 1 orange. Remove orange segments from both oranges. Add rind, segments, raisins and ginger to cranberry mixture. Simmer, stirring frequently 25 minutes. Add nuts, pour into sterilized jars and seal. Makes about 6 half-pints.

GEORGIA PEACH CONSERVE

- 4 pounds peaches (weigh after preparing)
- 1 cup nuts, chopped
- 6 3/4 cups sugar
- 2 oranges

Chop peaches into 1/2 inch cubes. Peel oranges, chop fruit and half the peel. Mix chopped peaches, orange pulp, peel, and sugar. Cook rapidly until mixture clears and reaches 220° on candy thermometer. Add nuts before removing from heat. Cool slightly. Process 5 minutes in hot water bath. Store in cool, dark place.

SWEET AND SOUR CHESTNUTS

1 pound chestnuts, shelled
4 cups water
2 cups sugar
2 lemons
1 small orange
4 whole cloves
1 cinnamon stick, 3 inches long
¼ teaspoon ginger
½ cup white raisins
½ cup almonds, whole

In saucepan combine water and sugar, bring to boil. Cut rind of lemons and orange into thin slivers, add to boiling syrup. Reduce heat to simmer. Add juice of 1 lemon and remaining lemon and orange, with white underskin cut off, sliced thin. Add spices and chestnuts. Simmer 45 minutes, stirring from time to time. Add raisins, cook 10 minutes more. Add almonds, cook 5 minutes longer. Pour into sterilized jars, seal, cool. Use as preserves or with pork, duck, goose or ham.

Vegetables

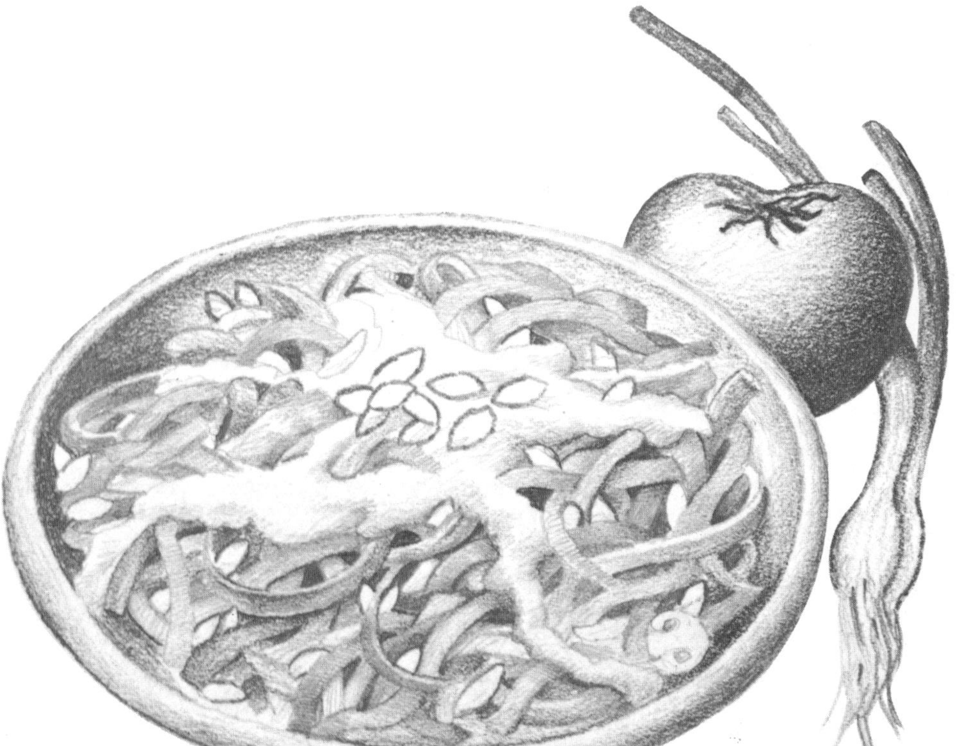

Vegetables

To dress up any vegetable dish, add a sprinkling of almonds.

ARTICHOKES SUPREME

Serves 8

3 14 ounce cans artichoke hearts, drained
1 cup butter or oleo, melted
2 4 ounce cans mushrooms, drained
½ cup lemon juice
1 2 ounce jar pimientos, chopped
½ teaspoon Italian seasoning
Salt and pepper to taste
½ cup almonds, slivered
Paprika

Preheat oven to 350°. Combine all ingredients except almonds and paprika in buttered casserole. Top with almonds, sprinkle with paprika. Bake til bubbly. Serve immediately.

ASPARAGUS ALMOND BAKE

Serves 4

1 14½ ounce can asparagus
½ cup potato chips, crushed
⅓ cup almonds, chopped
1 can cream of mushroom soup

Preheat oven to 375°. In 1 quart casserole put layer of asparagus, layer of potato chips, layer almonds. Repeat. Pour soup over. Add a little milk to soup if necessary. Bake for 15 minutes.

ASPARAGUS ALMONDINE

Serves 6

2 packages frozen asparagus spears
⅓ cup butter or oleo
½ cup almonds, slivered
Juice of ½ lemon

Cook asparagus, drain. Arrange on warm serving dish. Combine remaining ingredients in saucepan. Heat til butter melts. Pour over asparagus. (Fresh, cooked asparagus may be used)

VEGETABLES

RITZY ASPARAGUS CASSEROLE

Serves 6

1 cup Ritz cracker crumbs
2 14½ cans cut asparagus, drained
1 cup sharp cheese, grated
¾ cup butter or oleo
1 cup toasted almonds, ground
1 cup milk

Butter a casserole and alternate layers of asparagus, cheese, crumbs, dotted butter and almonds. Pour milk in side of dish. Prepare at least 2 hours before baking or night before. Bake at 350° for 1 hour.

BROCCOLI CASSEROLE

Serves 4-6

1 roll garlic cheese
2 packages frozen chopped broccoli
¼ cup almonds, chopped
1 onion, chopped
¼ stick butter or oleo
1 can cream of mushroom soup
1 small can mushrooms, drained
Ritz cracker crumbs

Preheat oven to 350°. Cook broccoli just til thawed, drain. Blend soup and cheese. Cook onion in butter. Mix together all ingredients and put in buttered casserole dish. Top with cracker crumbs. Bake for 30 minutes.

SKILLET BROCCOLI AND CORN

Serves 4

4 tablespoons butter or oleo
1 10 ounce package frozen broccoli, thawed and chopped
1 10 ounce package frozen whole kernel corn
1 small can mushrooms, drained
3 tablespoons almonds, chopped
Salt and pepper

In skillet melt butter and add other ingredients. Saute 10 minutes, stirring often.

SPECIAL BRUSSEL SPROUTS

- **2 10 ounce packages frozen Brussel sprouts, cooked**
- **1 can cream of chicken soup**
- **1 small jar pimiento, chopped**
- **⅛ teaspoon thyme**
- **⅛ teaspoon pepper**
- **2 teaspoons butter or oleo**
- **½ cup almonds, chopped**

Serves 4

Preheat oven to 350°. Combine soup, pimiento, and seasonings, stir in Brussel sprouts. Put in 1½ quart buttered casserole. Melt butter, add almonds, cook 3 minutes. Spoon over casserole. Bake for 20 minutes.

Slice carrots diagonally and cook. Drain, mix with butter, brown sugar, and slivered almonds. Heat through.

CABBAGE-CARROT COMBO

- **1 beef bouillon cube**
- **1 large head cabbage, shredded**
- **4 carrots, grated**
- **½ cup green onions, sliced**
- **½ teaspoon salt**
- **¼ teaspoon pepper**
- **2 tablespoons butter or oleo, melted**
- **⅓ cup pecans, chopped**
- **1 teaspoon prepared mustard**
- **Paprika**

Serves 6-8

In large saucepan dissolve bouillon in ¼ cup water. Add cabbage, carrots, green onion, salt and pepper, toss to mix, cook, covered 5 to 10 minutes, stirring once. Combine butter, pecans, and mustard. Pour over vegetables, toss. Place in serving dish. Sprinkle with paprika.

SAVORY CARROTS WITH WALNUTS

Serves 12

3 pounds carrots
Salt
2 tablespoons green onions, sliced
½ cup butter or oleo, softened
1½ cups black walnuts or English walnuts, chopped

Cut carrots into julienne strips. In saucepan combine carrots, salt and onions in water, bring to a boil. Cover and simmer til tender, about 25 minutes. Drain. Toss with butter and walnuts. Season to taste. Serve warm. This may be made ahead and reheated.

CAULIFLOWER ONION BAKE

Serves 8

1 10 ounce package frozen cauliflower, thawed
2 10 ounce packages frozen onions in cream sauce
¾ cup Cheddar cheese, grated
¼ cup toasted almonds, slivered
1 tablespoon parsley
1 can French fried onions

Preheat oven to 350°. Cut cauliflower into bite-sized pieces. Prepare creamed onions according to package directions. Add cauliflower, cheese, almonds, and parsley. Put into 1½ quart casserole. Bake, uncovered for 35 minutes. Top with fried onions, bake 5 minutes more.

SAVORY CAULIFLOWER-PEA AMANDINE

Serves 6

2 10 ounce packages frozen cauliflower, cooked and drained
1 10 ounce package frozen peas, cooked and drained
2 tablespoons butter or oleo
1½ cups sour cream
1 teaspoon onion salt
1 teaspoon curry powder
½ cup slivered almonds

Preheat oven to 325°. In saucepan, melt butter, add flour, stir til smooth. Cook and stir 1 minute. Add sour cream and stir til just hot. Add onion salt, combine with cauliflower and peas in 1½ quart casserole. Melt 1 tablespoon butter in saucepan, stir in curry powder and almonds. Cook and stir 3 minutes. Put on top of casserole. Bake for 25 minutes.

CELERY PECAN CASSEROLE

Serves 4

3 cups celery, diced
1 tablespoon sugar
1 cup pecan halves
½ stick butter or oleo
3 tablespoons flour
½ pint light cream
1 teaspoon salt
½ teaspoon red pepper
1 egg, well beaten
Ritz cracker crumbs

In saucepan cover celery with water and cook with sugar til tender, drain. Mix celery with pecans. Melt butter, add flour, cook and stir for 2 minutes. Gradually add milk, stir til thick. Add salt, red pepper and egg. Mix with celery and nuts. Pour into buttered 1½ quart casserole, top with crumbs. Bake for 30 minutes.

SCRUMPTIOUS CELERY

Serves 6

4 cups celery, sliced in 2 inch pieces
1 medium onion, sliced
2 tablespoons butter or oleo
⅓ cup whole blanched almonds
1 chicken bouillon cube
½ teaspoon sugar
⅛ teaspoon each garlic powder and ginger

Saute onions in butter til tender. Add remaining ingredients, cover, cook over medium heat 10 minutes, stirring often. Serve hot.

EGGPLANT CASSEROLE

Serves 6

1 medium eggplant
Salt and pepper
1 egg, beaten
1 cup Italian style croutons, crushed
2 cups Mozzarella cheese, grated
¾ cup almonds, chopped

Preheat oven to 375°. Peel eggplant, cut in ½ inch slices. Salt and pepper. Dip each slice in egg, then in bread crumbs. Put slices in buttered baking dish. Bake for 15 minutes. Sprinkle cheese and almonds over. Bake 5 more minutes.

COMPANY GREEN BEANS

Serves 10-12

3 16 ounce cans French style green beans, drained
1 small onion, chopped
1 can cream of celery soup
1 can cream of mushroom soup
1 small can mushrooms
½ cup almonds, chopped
Salt and pepper
1 can French fried onions

Preheat oven to 325°. Combine all ingredients except fried onions in casserole. Bake for 30 minutes. Put onion rings on top. Bake 15 more minutes.

FAST GREEN BEANS

Serves 8

2 16 ounce cans French style green beans, drained
1 can Cheddar cheese soup
½ cup almonds, slivered

Preheat oven to 350°. Add green beans to Cheddar cheese soup in baking dish. Top with almonds. Bake for 30 minutes.

GREEN BEANS AMANDINE

Serves 6

¼ cup almonds, slivered
¼ cup butter or oleo
½ teaspoon salt
2 tablespoons lemon juice
2 16 ounce cans French style green beans

Heat green beans, drain, put in serving dish. In saucepan cook almonds in butter til golden. Remove from heat, add lemon juice and salt. Pour over green beans.

LIMA BEAN CASSEROLE

Serves 6-8

1 large can lima beans
2 beef bouillon cubes
1 medium onion, chopped
Dash Worcestershire
½ cup mild cheese, grated
½ cup pecans, chopped
Bread crumbs
Butter or oleo

Preheat oven to 350°. Drain beans, reserve liquid. Heat liquid and dissolve bouillon cubes. Add onions and Worcestershire. Alternate layers of beans, cheese, and pecans in buttered 1 quart casserole. Pour onion mixture over each layer. Cover with crumbs and dot with butter. Bake for 35 minutes.

GOURMET NOODLES

Serves 4

½ cup butter or oleo, melted
½ pound fresh mushrooms, sliced
¼ cup onion, chopped
¼ cup almonds, sliced
1 clove garlic, minced
1 10½ ounce can beef consomme
1 tablespoon lemon juice
4 ounces medium noodles

In large saucepan combine butter, mushrooms, onion, almonds and garlic. Cook 10 minutes over low heat. Add remaining ingredients. Cook til noodles are tender, about 10 minutes.

NUTTY NOODLES

Serves 8-10

4 tablespoons butter or oleo
1 small onion, chopped
1 medium can mushrooms
2 cans consomme
1 10 ounce package noodles
1 cup almonds, slivered

Saute onion and mushroom in 2 tablespoons butter. Add consomme and mushroom juice. Bring to boil. Add noodles and cook til liquid is absorbed. Saute almonds in remaining butter and mix into noodles.

NOODLES WITH PECANS

Serves 6

¼ cup bread crumbs
½ cup pecans, chopped
6 tablespoons butter or oleo, melted
1 8 ounce package egg noodles
Salt
1 tablespoon dry sherry
2 tablespoons parsley

Cook noodles in boiling, salted water, drain. In skillet toss bread crumbs and pecans with 3 tablespoons butter. Saute over medium heat until lightly toasted. Toss noodles with remaining butter, sherry, parsley, and salt to taste. Put in 2 quart casserole, cover with crumbs and pecans. Serve at once or keep warm in 250°oven 5 to 10 minutes.

BAKED ONIONS

Serves 6

2 pounds white boiling onions
5 tablespoons butter or oleo
3 tablespoons flour
1 cup water
1 tablespoon brown sugar
1 teaspoon salt
1 teaspoon Worcestershire
Dash pepper
¼ teaspoon paprika
2 tablespoons toasted almonds

Preheat oven to 375°. Peel onions, boil in salted water 20 minutes, drain. Put in 1 quart casserole. In saucepan melt butter, blend in flour. Stir in water, brown sugar, salt, Worcestershire, and pepper. Cook til slightly thickened. Pour over onions. Sprinkle with paprika. Cover and bake for 20 minutes. Just before serving, sprinkle with almonds.

SCALLOPED ONIONS

Serves 6

2 pounds white boiling onions
1 can cream of chicken soup
½ cup American cheese, grated
¼ cup almonds, chopped

Preheat oven to 375°. Peel onions, boil in salted water 20 minutes, drain. Place in baking dish, add soup. Top with cheese and almonds. Bake for 30 minutes.

CREAMED PEA SURPRISE

Serves 8-10

1 stick butter or oleo
1 medium onion, chopped
1 can cream of chicken soup
1 cup sharp cheese, grated
4 hard boiled eggs, chopped
⅓ cup almonds, chopped
1 small can mushrooms
2 cups green peas, drained
potato chips

Preheat oven to 300°. Saute onion in butter and stir in soup, cheese, eggs, almonds, and mushrooms, mixing well. Add peas and pour into buttered 2 quart casserole. Bake for 20 to 30 minutes. Cover with crushed potato chips last 5 minutes.

Bake potatoes. Slice thru middle lengthwise, scoop out and mash; mix with blue cheese dip. Heap back into shells and garnish with almonds. Put in oven to heat through.

PEA PODS WITH ALMONDS

Serves 4

¼ cup green onions, chopped
2 tablespoons butter or oleo
1 6 ounce frozen pea pods, thawed
1 cup fresh mushrooms, sliced
2 teaspoons cornstarch
⅔ cup cold water
1 teaspoon instant chicken bouillon granules
2 teaspoons soy sauce
2 tablespoons toasted almonds, slivered

In skillet cook onion in butter til tender. Add pea pods and mushrooms, toss and cook on high 1 minute. Remove from heat. Combine cornstarch and cold water. Stir cornstarch mixture, bouillon granules, and soy sauce into pea pods and mushrooms. Cook and stir until mixture thickens and bubbles. Toss with almonds.

EASY ALMOND RICE

Serves 6

½ stick butter or oleo
1 cup rice
1 can beef consomme
1 can water
⅓ cup almonds, sliced

Preheat oven to 350°. Brown rice in butter, add consomme and water. Steam a few minutes. Add almonds, pour into casserole, bake for ½ hour, cover, continue baking 45 more minutes.

PEANUT RICE

Cook 4 servings of rice, drain and mix with 2 tablespoons melted butter. Stir in ¼ to ⅓ cup salted peanuts, chopped. Serve with boiled ham.

RICE SUPREME

Serves 6

2 cups chicken broth
1 teaspoon salt
1 tablespoon lemon juice
½ teaspoon dry tarragon
1 cup rice
¼ cup mushrooms
¼ cup butter or oleo, melted
Pepper
¼ cup dry sherry
2 tablespoons parsley
½ cup toasted almonds and filberts, chopped

Bring broth to boil, remove from heat, stir in salt, lemon juice, tarragon, and rice. Bring to boil. Cover and simmer over low heat til liquid is absorbed. Saute mushrooms in butter, add pepper, sherry, and parsley. Add mushroom mixture to rice and toss. Spoon into serving dish, top with almonds.

WILD RICE WITH ALMONDS

Serves 6-8

1 cup wild rice
¼ cup butter or oleo
½ cup almonds, slivered
2 tablespoons chives
1 8 ounce can mushrooms
3 cups chicken broth

Preheat oven to 325°. Wash and drain rice. In skillet add rice to butter with almonds, chives and mushrooms. Cook and stir until almonds are golden. Pour rice mixture into ungreased 1½ quart casserole. Heat chicken broth to boiling, stir into rice mixture. Cover tightly, bake for 1½ hours.

ADA GUNN'S SQUASH CASSEROLE

Serves 6

5 yellow squash, sliced
1 medium onion, chopped
1 can mushroom soup
2 eggs, beaten
8 ounces Cheddar cheese, grated
½ cup pecans, chopped
1 teaspoon salt
¾ cup Ritz cracker crumbs

Preheat oven to 350°. Boil squash and onion together til tender, drain. Combine soup, salt, eggs, and cheese. Mix with squash and onions, add pecans. Put in 1½ quart baking dish. Top with cracker crumbs. Bake for 30 minutes.

ORANGE-PECAN STUFFED SQUASH

Serves 4

2 acorn squash
1 tablespoon brown sugar
1 tablespoon butter or oleo
¼ teaspoon salt
¼ teaspoon orange peel, grated
2 tablespoons pecans, chopped

Preheat oven to 350°. Halve squash, remove seeds. Place, cut side down, on greased baking sheet. Bake for 35 minutes. Scoop out pulp. Stir together pulp, brown sugar, butter, salt, and orange peel. Add a little orange juice to make fluffy. Refill shells, sprinkle with pecans. Bake for 10 minutes.

SAVORY SWEET POTATOES

Serves 6

6 sweet potatoes, baked
Salt
½ cup brown sugar
1 tablespoon cornstarch
1 cup orange juice
¼ cup raisins
¼ cup butter or oleo, melted
2 tablespoons walnuts, chopped

Preheat oven to 350°. Halve sweet potatoes, place in baking dish, sprinkle with salt. Combine sugar, cornstarch, and ¼ teaspoon salt. Gradually add orange juice, blending well. Quickly bring to boil, stirring constantly. Add raisins, butter, and walnuts, mix well. Pour over potatoes. Bake uncovered for 20 minutes.

SWEET POTATO BALLS

Serves 8

4 large sweet potatoes
1 cup pecans, chopped
1 cup corn flakes, crushed
1 tablespoon flour
¾ cup sugar
2 tablespoons milk
1 teaspoon cinnamon
1 teaspoon vanilla
Bourbon to taste
¼ teaspoon baking powder
Large marshmallows, halved
Cooking oil

Peel, slice and boil potatoes til done, drain, mash til smooth. Add rest of ingredients except marshmallows and oil, mix well. Chill. Mold sweet potatoes around marshmallow halves, shape each into ball, roll in additional corn flakes. Refrigerate to set. Fry in deep fat at 375° for 3 or 4 minutes. Drain well.

SWEET POTATO DELIGHT

Serves 8-10

6 sweet potatoes, cooked (or 1 large can yams)
6 tablespoons butter or oleo
3 eggs, slightly beaten
½ cup sugar
½ cup pecans, chopped
½ cup coconut, flaked
½ cup orange juice
½ teaspoon salt
½ teaspoon vanilla
10 orange slices
10 marshmallows

Preheat oven to 350°. Mash potatoes, stir in butter. Beat in eggs, sugar, pecans, coconut, orange juice, salt, and vanilla. Put into 1½ quart casserole. Bake, uncovered for 30 minutes. Top with orange slices. Put one marshmallow on each orange slice. Return to oven till marshmallows are golden brown.

CREAMY SPINACH CASSEROLE

Serves 6-8

2 10 ounce packages frozen chopped spinach
1 3 ounce cream cheese
¼ cup butter or oleo
Salt and pepper
¼ cup Parmesan cheese, grated
½ cup pecans, chopped

Preheat oven to 350°. Cook spinach in salted water, drain. Melt cheese and butter together, add to spinach. Pour into buttered casserole, top with Parmesan cheese and pecans. Bake til bubbly, about 30 minutes.

SOUTH PACIFIC COCONUT SPINACH

Serves 4

2 10 ounce packages frozen chopped spinach, thawed and drained
½ cup coconut milk
Salt and pepper
1 small onion, chopped
½ cup coconut, crushed

In top of double boiler combine spinach with coconut milk. Cook covered for 25 minutes. Add salt and pepper to taste. Stir in half the onion and half the coconut. Put into heated serving dish. Top with remaining onion and coconut.

VEGETABLE RAMEKINS

Serves 6

1 medium onion, chopped
1 tablespoon butter or oleo
1 can cream of celery soup
1 teaspoon Worcestershire
¼ cup nuts, chopped
1 1 pound can peas, drained
1 1 pound can cut green beans, drained
1 small jar pimientos, diced
1 cup buttered bread crumbs

Preheat oven to 350°. Cook onion in butter til tender. Stir in all ingredients except bread crumbs. Put into ramekins or individual shallow baking dishes. Sprinkle with crumbs. Bake for 25 minutes.

YUMMY YAMS

Serves 6-8

2 apples, sliced
⅓ cup pecans, chopped
½ cup brown sugar
½ teaspoon cinnamon
2 17 ounce cans yams, drained
¼ cup butter or oleo
1 cup miniature marshmallows

Preheat oven to 350°. Toss apples and nuts with brown sugar and cinnamon. Alternate layers of apples and yams in 1½ quart casserole. Dot with butter. Cover, bake for 35 minutes. Put marshmallows on top. Return to oven til browned.

STIR-FRY ZUCCHINI

Serves 4

¼ cup whole blanched almonds
¼ cup butter or oleo
1 teaspoon salt
½ teaspoon onion powder
¼ teaspoon pepper
1 pound zucchini, sliced

In skillet roast almonds in butter, add salt, onion powder, pepper, and zucchini. Cook, stirring, about 15 minutes.

Main Course

Main Course

ALMOND STUFFED GREEN PEPPERS

6 green peppers
⅓ cup toasted almonds, chopped
3 cups cooked rice
1 teaspoon salt
Dash pepper
1 tablespoon onion, grated
1 cup American cheese, grated

Serves 6

Preheat oven to 350°. Cut tops from peppers, remove membranes, cover with water and boil 5 minutes, drain. Mix remaining ingredients, fill peppers, dot with butter. Bake for 30 minutes.

CHEESE-WALNUT LOAF

4 eggs, beaten
1 pound Cheddar cheese, grated
1½ cups walnuts, chopped
1 cup cooked brown rice
½ cup quick-cooking rolled oats
½ cup fresh mushrooms, chopped
1 medium onion, chopped
1 clove garlic, minced
¼ teaspoon salt
⅛ teaspoon pepper

Mushroom Sauce:
⅓ cup butter or oleo, melted
½ pound fresh mushrooms, sliced
3 tablespoons flour
½ teaspoon salt
Dash cayenne
2 cups milk

Serves 6-8

Preheat oven to 350°. Combine all ingredients except for mushroom sauce in bowl, mix well. Put in greased loaf pan. Bake for 50 minutes. Remove, let stand 10 minutes. Turn out on warm serving dish. Make mushroom sauce while loaf is in oven. Saute mushrooms in butter, stir in flour, salt, and cayenne. Gradually stir in milk and cook and stir until thickened. Pour over loaf on serving dish.

GEORGIA PINTO-BEAN LOAF

Serves 6

1 16 ounce package dry pinto beans
1 small onion, sliced
1 clove garlic, crushed
1 8 ounce can tomato sauce
1 cup carrot, grated
1 cup cooked rice
½ cup celery, diced
2 eggs, slightly beaten
¼ cup blanched almonds, chopped
2 teaspoons salt
¼ teaspoon pepper
Sour cream

Prepare pinto beans with onion and garlic according to quick-cook directions on package. When fully cooked, drain, mash beans with potato masher. Stir in remaining ingredients except sour cream. Put into greased oblong baking dish. Bake at 375° for 1 hour 15 minutes. Let stand 5 minutes. Invert onto warm dish. Slice and serve with sour cream.

BEEF CASSEROLE DELUXE

Serves 6 to 8

2 medium onions, chopped
1½ pounds ground beef
3 tablespoons butter or oleo
2 10½ ounce cans tomato soup
1 3 ounce cream cheese
2 tablespoons sugar
2 teaspoons salt
1½ tablespoons Worcestershire
¼ teaspoon pepper
1 8 ounce box wide noodles, cooked
1 cup whole mushrooms
1 cup corn flakes, crushed
¾ cup almonds, chopped
1 teaspoon salt

Preheat oven to 350°. Cook onions and meat in butter til brown. Add soup, cream cheese, sugar, Worcestershire, salt and pepper. Simmer 15 minutes. Pour over noodles in greased baking dish. Top with mushrooms and corn flakes. Bake for 20 minutes. A few minutes before removing sprinkle almonds over top.

BEEF LUNCHEON SALAD

Serves 12

2 cups boiled new potatoes, sliced
1 cup green onions, sliced
2 cups celery and tops, chopped
3 cups lean boiled beef, sliced and cut in 1½ inch squares
12 slices sour pickles
1 cup cherry tomatoes
¼ cup capers
½ cup green pepper strips
Salad greens
6 hard boiled eggs
3 tablespoons Dijon mustard
1 cup olive oil
1½ teaspoon garlic salt
1 teaspoon black pepper
⅓ cup vinegar
Dash Tabasco
Walnuts, chopped

Combine potatoes, onions, celery, beef, pickles, tomatoes, capers and green pepper. Toss, arrange on greens. Combine yolks of 3 eggs with mustard. Stir in olive oil, salt, pepper and vinegar. Add Tabasco. Pour over beef. Garnish salad with rest of eggs, quartered, walnuts and chopped egg whites.

CURRIED BEEF LOAF

Serves 8

2 pounds ground beef
1 cup onion, chopped
2 tablespoons curry powder
1 tablespoon sugar
1 teaspoon salt
⅛ teaspoon pepper
1½ cups bread crumbs
2 eggs, beaten
½ cup milk
½ cup raisins
½ cup blanched almonds, chopped
2 tablespoons vinegar
4 bay leaves
3 eggs, beaten
⅔ cup milk
⅛ teaspoon salt
Dash pepper

Preheat oven to 350°. In large skillet, cook ground beef, onion, and curry, stirring to brown meat. Pour off grease, remove from heat. Add sugar, salt and pepper. Stir in bread crumbs, the first 2 eggs, ½ cup milk, raisins, almonds, vinegar, and bay leaves. Pack mixture into 9x9x2 inch baking pan. Combine the remaining 3 eggs, ⅔ cup milk, salt and pepper, beat til blended. Slowly pour over top of meat mixture. Bake uncovered at 350° for 45 minutes or til egg mixture is set and lightly browned.

HAWAIIAN BEEF DINNER

Serves 6

2 pounds boneless beef chuck, cut in 1½ inch cubes
1 tablespoon fat
1 small onion, chopped
1 clove garlic, crushed
1 teaspoon salt
½ teaspoon ginger
1 20 ounce can pineapple chunks
1 beef bouillon cube
¼ cup brown sugar
¼ cup vinegar
2 tablespoons cornstarch
1 tablespoon molasses
1 9 ounce package frozen cut green beans, cooked and drained
2 bananas, cut in ¾ inch chunks
2 tablespoons honey
½ cup toasted coconut, grated
Hot cooked rice

Brown beef in fat. Add onion, garlic, onion, garlic, salt, and ginger. Drain pineapple, reserving liquid. Add water to make 1½ cups. Add ½ cup to meat, bring to boil, cover and simmer 2 hours. In saucepan mix remaining liquid, pineapple, bouillon cube, sugar, vinegar, and cornstarch. Bring to boil, cook, stirring, til thickened. Arrange meat in mounds at opposite ends of large pyrex dish. Arrange beans and pineapple between mounds. Drizzle sauce over all. Add banana, drizzle on honey, sprinkle with coconut. Bake at 350° for 5 minutes. Serve with rice.

PECAN STUFFED MEAT LOAF

Serves 6

1½ pounds ground chuck
1½ cups bread crumbs
½ cup green pepper, chopped
¾ cup onion, chopped
1 tablespoon Worcestershire
1 teaspoon salt
⅓ cup milk
2 eggs
½ cup celery, chopped
½ cup pecans, chopped
¼ teaspoon pepper
⅓ cup meat stock

Preheat oven to 350°. Combine meat, crumbs, green pepper, onion, Worcestershire, salt, milk and eggs, mix thoroughly. Place ½ in greased loaf loaf pan. Mix remaining ingredients together, place on top of meat. Put remaining meat mixture on top. Bake at 350° for 1½ hours.

BAKED VEAL CUTLETS

Serves 6

6 veal cutlets
1 egg, beaten
½ pint sour cream
1 cup flour
1 teaspoon baking powder
2 teaspoons salt
¼ teaspoon pepper
2 teaspoons paprika
¼ cup pecans, chopped
2 tablespoons sesame seeds
½ cup butter or oleo

Preheat oven to 400°. Dip veal into egg mixed with sour cream, then into mixture of flour, baking powder, salt, pepper, paprika, pecans and sesame seeds. Melt butter in pan in oven, place veal in single layer in pan, turn once to coat with butter. Bake for 30 minutes, turn, bake 30 more minutes.

VEAL WITH PISTACHIO STUFFING

Serves 8

1 3 pound slice of veal, cut from leg
½ pound chicken livers
¾ pound ham
½ cup pistachios, chopped
1 teaspoon salt
½ cup butter or oleo, melted
¼ teaspoon allspice
¼ teaspoon thyme
¼ teaspoon pepper
Flour
Salt and pepper
4 strips bacon

Preheat oven to 325°. Have butcher cut piece of veal you need. Have him take bone out and pound the meat into a single, wide cutlet that can be rolled. Cut half the chicken livers into small pieces, put the rest through meat grinder with ham. Combine nuts, salt, butter, allspice, thyme, pepper and cut livers, blend. Spread over veal and roll like jelly roll. Tie securely. Dredge with flour and sprinkle lightly with salt and pepper. Place 2 strips of bacon in bottom of roasting pan. Lay veal on top, cover with rest of bacon strips. Bake 2 hours, basting often. When done, cool, then chill. Remove string before serving. Serve with halved hard boiled eggs, spread with mayonnaise. Garnish with watercress.

MAIN COURSE

HAM SALAD CASSEROLE

2 cups ham, chopped
1 cup celery, chopped
½ cup pecans, chopped
1 tablespoon onion, chopped
¼ cup sweet pickle relish
1 teaspoon salt
1 cup mayonnaise
½ cup Cheddar cheese, grated
1 cup potato chips, crushed

Serves 4
Preheat oven to 400°. Mix together ham, celery, pecans, onions, relish, salt and mayonnaise in baking dish. Sprinkle with cheese and potato chips. Bake for 20 minutes.

SAVORY SAUSAGE CASSEROLE

1 pound bulk pork sausage
1 cup uncooked rice
2 2 ounce packages dehydrated chicken noodle soup
¼ cup onion, chopped
1 cup celery, chopped
2½ cups water
1 tablespoon soy sauce
½ cup almonds, slivered

Serves 4
Preheat oven to 350°. Brown sausage in skillet, pour off fat. Remove from heat. Mix together with remaining ingredients and place in casserole. Bake, covered, for 1 hour.

SWEET SPICY RIBS

3 pounds pork spareribs
2 tablespoons corn oil
1 cup dry sherry
1 large onion, chopped
½ cup water
½ cup light raisins
2 cloves garlic, minced
2 tablespoons sugar
2 teaspoons salt
¼ teaspoon pepper
¼ teaspoon ground cloves
2 tablespoons cold water
4 teaspoons cornstarch
¼ cup toasted almonds, slivered

Serves 4
Preheat oven to 350°. Cut meat in 2 or 3 rib portions. In dutch oven brown ribs in oil. Drain off excess fat. Return all ribs to pan. Remove pan from heat, add sherry, onion, ½ cup water, raisins, garlic, sugar, salt, pepper and cloves. Cover and cook at 350° for 1½ hours. Remove ribs, blend cold water and cornstarch into drippings in pan. Cook and stir til bubbly. Stir in almonds. Serve sauce with ribs.

Nuts enrich the flavor of chicken, turkey, veal, fish and duckling.

ALMOND FRIED CHICKEN

Serves 6

1 frying chicken, cut up
1 cup flour
2 teaspoons salt
¼ teaspoon pepper
2 teaspoons paprika
2 eggs, slightly beaten
2 tablespoons milk
1½ cups almonds, finely chopped
2 tablespoons butter or oleo
2 tablespoons shortening

Preheat oven to 400°. Combine flour, salt, pepper, and paprika in paper bag. Toss chicken in mixture. Dip chicken one piece at a time in eggs mixed with milk. Roll in almonds. Let stand for 5 or 10 minutes. Melt butter and shortening in shallow baking dish in oven. Place coated chicken skin side down in dish. Bake for 30 minutes, turn chicken over, bake about 30 more minutes.

BAKED ALMOND CHICKEN AND RICE

Serves 6

3 whole chicken breasts
¾ cup light cream
¾ cup almonds, ground
1 teaspoon white pepper
⅛ teaspoon thyme
½ can cream of mushroom soup
1 cup water
1 cup milk
2 cups cooked rice
¼ cup pimiento, chopped
2 tablespoons butter or oleo

Preheat oven to 350°. Remove skin and bones and cut chicken in half. Dip in cream, then in mixture of almonds, salt, pepper and thyme. Mix soup with water, bring to boil, add milk, rice and pimientos. Spread in greased 8x12 inch baking dish. Arrange chicken over it and dot with butter. Bake for 45 minutes.

CHICKEN TETRAZZINI

Serves 6 to 8

1 4 to 4½ pound hen
1 cup celery, chopped
1 large onion, chopped
1 green pepper, chopped
4 cans cream of mushroom soup
2 cloves garlic
1 cup toasted almonds, slivered
1 16 ounce package thin spaghetti

Cover chicken with water and simmer til tender, cool. Cut chicken into bite size pieces. Save broth, cook celery, onion, pepper, garlic and spaghetti in broth, drain. Add chicken, mushroom soup and almonds. Put into casserole, sprinkle with grated cheese. Bake at 350° for 30 minutes.

Chicken croquettes rolled in chopped almonds or pecans before cooking become a party entrée!

HAWAIIAN LUNCHEON

Serves 24

6 large fresh pineapples
7½ cups cooked chicken, cubed
2½ cups celery, diced
2½ cups bananas, sliced
1 cup almonds, slivered
2½ cups mayonnaise
6 tablespoons chutney or 1½ teaspoon salt
2 teaspoons curry powder
1½ cups coconut, shredded
3 11 ounce cans mandarin oranges

Leave green tops on pineapple and cut pineapples into fourths, lengthwise. Cut around edges with knife, remove fruit and cube. Drain fruit and shells on paper towels. Mix pineapple, chicken, celery, bananas and nuts. Blend mayonnaise, chutney, and curry powder. Carefully toss mayonnaise mixture with pineapple mixture. Fill each pineapple shell with fruit mixture. Sprinkle with coconut. Garnish top with mandarin orange sections.

HOT CHICKEN SALAD

Serves 4

- 1 5 ounce can boned chicken
- 1 can cream of chicken soup
- 1 cup celery, chopped
- 1 tablespoon lemon juice
- ½ cup almonds, slivered
- ¾ cup mayonnaise
- ½ teaspoon pepper
- ½ cup Cheddar or Swiss cheese, grated
- 1 small bag potato chips, crushed

Preheat oven to 400°. Combine all ingredients except potato chips. Put in casserole, cover with potato chips. Bake at 400° for 20 minutes.

IN A HURRY!

Serve 4

- 1 can boned chicken
- 2 cans cream of chicken soup
- 1 small can mushrooms
- ½ cup toasted almonds
- 4 slices buttered toast

Combine and heat chicken, soup, mushrooms and almonds. Serve over toast points.

INDIAN RICE

Serves 4

- 1 cup rice
- 4 tablespoons raisins
- 2 tablespoons toasted almonds
- ½ teaspoon curry powder
- 2 cups chicken, cooked and chopped

Preheat oven to 350°. Prepare rice according to directions on package. Stir in remaining ingredients except chicken. Cover and bake for 10 minutes. Remove from oven and stir in chicken. Bake 10 more minutes.

STIR-FRY CHICKEN

Serves 4

- 1 teaspoon ginger
- 2 whole chicken breasts
- 2 teaspoons sugar
- 1 tablespoon cornstarch
- 3 teaspoons water
- 3 teaspoons soy sauce
- ⅓ cup sherry
- 1 cup whole almonds
- ¼ cup corn oil
- 2 6 ounce packages Chinese pea pods, thawed

Skin, bone, and cut chicken in ½ inch cubes. In bowl mix ginger, sugar, and cornstarch. Blend in water, soy sauce and sherry. In wok or skillet add almonds to oil, stir and cook 3 minutes. Add chicken, cook til meat turns white. Pour in sherry mixture, cook til sauce thickens. Add pea pods, stir-fry til hot and glazed.

STIR-FRY CHICKEN II

Serves 4-6

- 1 cup walnuts
- ¼ cup salad oil
- 2 whole chicken breasts
- 1 cup onion, sliced
- 1½ cups celery, sliced
- ½ cup chicken broth
- 1 tablespoon cornstarch
- 1 teaspoon sugar
- ¼ cup soy sauce
- 2 tablespoons dry sherry
- ¾ cup chicken broth
- 1 5 ounce can bamboo shoots
- 1 5 ounce can water chestnuts, sliced

In skillet or wok toast nuts in salad oil, drain on paper towels. Skin, bone, and cut chicken in thin strips. Add to skillet, sprinkle with salt, cook til meat is white. Remove. Add onion, celery, and broth to skillet. Cook 5 minutes. Combine cornstarch, sugar, soy sauce, sherry and broth. Pour over vegetables, cook til sauce thickens. Add chicken, bamboo shoots, water chestnuts and toasted nuts. Heat through. Serve with rice.

YUMMY CHICKEN

Serves 4

- 1 chicken, cut up
- ½ cup butter or oleo, melted
- 2 teaspoons dried onion
- 1 tablespoon parsley
- ¼ cup almonds, chopped
- ¼ cup Parmesan cheese
- 1 cup bread crumbs
- 1 teaspoon salt

Preheat oven to 350°. Combine butter and onions. Combine parsley, almonds, cheese, crumbs and salt. Dip chicken pieces in butter mixture, then in crumb mixture. Put in baking dish. Cover. Bake for 1 hour.

CORNISH HENS WITH WILD RICE

Serves 4

1 6 ounce package long-grain and wild rice mix
¼ cup raisins
2 tablespoons butter or oleo
2 tablespoons blanched almonds, slivered
½ teaspoon rubbed sage
4 Rock Cornish game hens
4 tablespoons butter or oleo, melted

Preheat oven to 400°. Cook rice according to package directins; stir in raisins, butter, almonds and sage. Salt cavities of hens. Fill each with about ¾ cup stuffing, cover opening with a piece of foil. Tie wings to body, tie legs to tail. Brush with melted butter. Cook covered at 400° for 20 minutes. Reduce heat to 325°, cook 30 more minutes. Uncover, bake 10 more minutes to brown.

TOKYO TURKEY

Serves 6

2 cups cooked turkey, cubed
1 16 ounce can bean sprouts, drained
1 cup cooked rice
1 cup celery, chopped
1 cup carrot, grated
2 tablespoons green pepper, chopped
¼ cup French dressing
2 tablespoons soy sauce
¼ teaspoon salt
Dash pepper
½ cup mayonnaise
½ cup toasted almonds, slivered

Combine all ingredients except mayonnaise and almonds. Chill. Just before serving, stir in mayonnaise and almonds. Mix well. Serve on lettuce.

TURKEY CRUNCH CASSEROLE

Serves 6

3 cups cooked turkey, diced
2 hard cooked eggs, chopped
1 small can mushrooms
¾ cup celery, chopped
½ cup blanched almonds, slivered
1 tablespoon onion, chopped
1 can cream of chicken soup
¾ cup mayonnaise
Chow mein noodles

Preheat oven to 350°. Mix together turkey, eggs, mushrooms, celery, almonds and onions. Stir soup into mayonnaise. Toss with turkey mixture. Put into 2 quart casserole. Sprinkle with noodles. Bake for 30 minutes.

TURKEY DIVAN

Serves 4-6

2 cups turkey, cubed
2 packages frozen broccoli spears, cooked and drained
6 slices American cheese
½ cup almonds, slivered
1 13½ ounce can evaporated milk
1 can cream of mushroom soup
1 can French fried onions

Preheat oven to 350°. Arrange turkey in oblong baking dish. Top with hot broccoli, cover with cheese and almonds. Stir together soup and milk, pour over cheese. Bake uncovered for 25 minutes. Cover with onion rings, bake 5 more minutes.

ORANGE-WALNUT STUFFED DUCK

Serves 3 to 4

3½ cups 1 inch bread cubes
½ cup hot water
1 egg, beaten
1½ teaspoons salt
Dash of pepper
¼ teaspoon poultry seasoning
½ cup toasted walnuts, chopped
2 tablespoons orange peel, grated
Pulp of 1 large orange
1¾ cups celery, sliced
¼ cup butter, melted
1 4 to 5 pound duck

Preheat oven to 350°. Toast bread cubes at 350° til brown. Pour hot water over, let stand for 10 minutes. Beat egg with ½ teaspoon salt, pepper and poultry seasoning, combine with nuts, bread, orange peel, orange pulp and celery. Pour butter over all, toss well. Rub inside of duck with 1 teaspoon salt, spoon in stuffing. Bake, uncovered, at 325° for 2 to 2½ hours. Garnish with orange slices.

SOFT SHELL CRABS AMANDINE

Serves 8

10 soft-shell crabs, cleaned
1¼ cups almonds, slivered
1 cup butter, clarified
2 tablespoons butter or oleo
½ cup flour
Juice of ½ lemon, strained
Salt and pepper

Rinse crabs under cold running water, drain on paper towels, patting to dry thoroughly. Clarify butter by heating butter slowly in small heavy pan. Remove white foam as it forms on top. Pour off clear, melted butter keeping back sediment. Heat the 2 tablespoons butter in heavy skillet over low heat, saute almonds til golden brown. Set aside. Dredge crabs with flour, shake off excess. Heat clarified butter over medium heat, saute crabs til just brown on both sides, turning them once. Remove crabs to platter. Add lemon juice to skillet, blend. Strain over crabs. Sprinkle lightly with salt and pepper. Scatter the almonds over crabs. Garnish with parsley and lemon wedges.

HOT CRABMEAT AVOCADO

Serves 6 to 8

1 7½ ounce can crabmeat
⅓ cup celery, chopped
3 hard cooked eggs, chopped
2 tablespoons pimiento, chopped
1 tablespoon onion, chopped
½ teaspoon salt
½ cup mayonnaise
3 large or 4 small ripe avocadoes
Lemon juice
Salt
3 tablespoons dry bread crumbs
1 teaspoon butter or oleo, melted
2 tablespoons slivered almonds

Preheat oven to 400°. Mix crabmeat, celery, egg, pimiento, onion, salt and mayonnaise. Cut unpeeled avocadoes in half lengthwise. Brush cut surface with lemon juice, sprinkle with salt. Fill avocado halves with crabmeat mixture. Toss bread crumbs with butter, spoon over top. Place in shallow baking dish. Bake uncovered 10 minutes. Sprinkle almonds over crumb topping. Bake 5 minutes longer or til filling is bubbly. Serve at once.

SCALLOP CASSEROLE SUPREME

4 tablespoons butter or oleo
5 tablespoons flour
1 cup light cream
½ teaspoon salt
¼ teaspoon red pepper
¾ cup sharp Cheddar cheese, grated
1 teaspoon onion juice
7 tablespoons sherry
1 pound scallops, steamed
1 can water chestnuts, sliced
1 14 ounce can artichoke hearts
1 cup almonds, slivered
¼ cup Parmesan cheese, grated

Serves 4

Preheat oven to 325°. Melt butter, add flour, combine well. Add cream, salt and red pepper, stirring constantly. Add cheese, cook until cheese melts. Stir in onion juice and sherry. Remove from heat. Spread scallops in buttered baking dish. Cover with water chestnuts then artichoke hearts then almonds. Pour sauce over, sprinkle with Parmesan cheese. Bake for 20 to 30 minutes.

OYSTER CASSEROLE

1 large onion, chopped
½ cup butter or oleo
3 cloves garlic, minced
2 tablespoons fresh parsley, chopped
½ teaspoon thyme
¼ teaspoon oregano
⅛ teaspoon red pepper
Salt and pepper to taste
4 dozen oysters
1 cup bread crumbs
2 slices bacon, fried and crumbled
10 almonds, crushed
Parmesan cheese, grated

Serves 4

Drain oysters, reserve juice. Set aside. Saute onion in butter til clear. Add garlic, parsley, seasonings and oysters. Cook til oysters curl at edges, add reserved juice. Fold in bread crumbs, bacon and almonds. Spoon into buttered casserole. Bake at 350° for 15 to 20 minutes.

MICROWAVE RED SNAPPER AMANDINE

Serves 4

1 pound red snapper, thawed or fresh
1 teaspoon lemon juice
Salt
⅓ cup almonds, slivered
⅓ cup butter or oleo

Put red snapper in 1½ quart glass baking dish. Rub lemon juice on top, salt lightly. Cover with plastic wrap. Microwave on HIGH for 6 to 7 minutes or til fish flakes easily. Keep covered while making sauce. In glass measuring cup combine almonds and butter. Microwave on HIGH for 2 minutes or til melted. Stir, continue cooking for 2 or 3 more minutes. Serve over fish.

SEAFOOD CHOW MEIN

Serves 6

1 cup celery, chopped
½ cup onion, chopped
2 tablespoons corn oil
2 cans cream of mushroom soup
½ cup water
1 cup peeled, deveined raw shrimp (or 2 9¼ ounce cans tuna)
1 can water chestnuts, sliced
½ pound crabmeat, flaked
1 cup almonds, chopped
1 3 ounce can chow mein noodles

Saute celery and onion in oil until tender, add soup, water, shrimp, water chestnuts and crabmeat. Put in Dutch oven. Sprinkle with almonds and noodles. Cover and place in cold oven. Bake at 350° for 1 hour.

MACADAMIA SHRIMP

Serves 4

1 cup water
½ pound shrimp, cleaned and shelled
½ teaspoon salt
½ teaspoon pepper
½ cup salted macadamia nuts, chopped
½ cup butter or oleo
6 tablespoons flour
1 tablespoon chili sauce
1½ cups milk
Hot cooked rice, noodles, or spaghetti

Bring water to boil, add shrimp, salt and pepper. Bring to boil again and cook 3 minutes. Drain, reserve liquid. Cook nuts in butter til lightly browned. Blend in flour. Add shrimp liquid, chili sauce and milk, cook, stirring til thickened. Add shrimp. Serve on rice. Filberts or almonds can be substituted.

SKILLET SHRIMP

Serves 4

1 can cream of shrimp frozen soup
¾ cup boiling water
½ cup celery, chopped
½ cup green pepper, chopped
1 package cooked frozen shrimp
⅔ cup minute rice
½ teaspoon salt
Dash Tabasco
Pepper
1½ teaspoon curry powder
½ cup ripe olives, sliced
2 tablespoons Parmesan cheese
2 tablespoons toasted almonds

In skillet place frozen soup, add boiling water. Cover, bring to a boil. Add celery, green pepper, shrimp, rice, salt, Tabasco and pepper. Simmer 10 to 15 minutes. Just before serving stir in olives and cheese. Sprinkle almonds on top.

TROUT AMANDINE

6 trout filets
1 cup milk
1 teaspoon salt
¼ teaspoon pepper
½ cup flour, sifted
¼ cup butter
½ cup almonds, slivered

Serves 4 to 6
Dip filets in milk, sprinkle with salt and pepper, roll in flour to coat. Melt butter in skillet, cook filets til brown. Remove fish from skillet. In same skillet, add almonds and saute. Sprinkle thickly over fish.

CHOPSTICK TUNA

1 can mushroom soup
¼ can water
1 3 ounce can chow mein noodles
1 7 ounce can tuna
1 cup celery, chopped
½ cup almonds, chopped
½ cup onion, chopped
Dash pepper
1 can peas, drained

Serves 4
Preheat oven to 350°. Combine soup and water. Add 1 cup noodles and remaining ingredients. Toss lightly. Place in baking dish. Sprinkle rest of noodles on top. Bake for 40 to 45 minutes.

TUNA NOODLE BAKE

1 8 ounce package noodles, cooked
1 can tuna
1 can cream of mushroom soup
¼ cup nuts, chopped
Ritz cracker crumbs

Serves 4
Preheat oven to 350°. Combine ingredients in casserole and put cracker crumbs on top. Bake for 30 minutes.

APPLE PECAN STUFFING

1 cup chicken broth
½ cup celery, chopped
¼ cup onion, chopped
4 tablespoons butter or oleo
½ teaspoon salt
4 cups whole wheat bread crumbs
2 medium apples, pared, cored, and chopped
½ cup pecans, chopped
1 teaspoon sage
¼ teaspoon cinnamon
⅛ teaspoon pepper

In saucepan combine broth, celery, onion, butter and salt. Bring to boil, cover, simmer 5 minutes. Combine crumbs, apples, pecans, sage, cinnamon and pepper in bowl. Pour broth mixture over, mix gently. Stuffs 8 to 10 pound turkey. Or put in 1½ quart casserole, bake, covered at 350° for 30 minutes.

BRAZIL NUT STUFFING

1 cup celery, chopped
¼ cup onion, chopped
¼ cup butter or oleo
2 7 ounce packages herb-seasoned stuffing mix
1 cup Brazil nuts, chopped
1 3 ounce can mushrooms, drained
3 cups hot milk

Cook onion and celery in butter til tender. Combine all ingredients, tossing lightly. Stuffs 10 to 12 pound turkey, 2 capons, or 2 large roasting chickens.

NEW ENGLAND CHESTNUT STUFFING

1 pound fresh chestnuts, chopped
1½ pounds ground beef
8 ounces pork sausage
1 cup onion, chopped
1 cup celery, chopped
3½ cups chicken broth
1 cup rice, uncooked
1 cup raisins
½ cup almonds, slivered (or pine nuts)
1½ teaspoon cinnamon
¼ teaspoon pepper
2 eggs, beaten

In skillet, brown beef with sausage, onion, and celery. Remove from heat, drain off fat. Add 3 cups broth, chestnuts, rice, raisins, almonds, salt, cinnamon, and pepper. Cover, simmer 30 minutes. Remove from heat. Combine ½ cup broth and eggs, stir into meat mixture. Stuffs 16-18 pound turkey. Or put into oblong pan, bake at 325° for 35 minutes.

PEANUT CELERY STUFFING

4 cups celery and leaves, chopped
2 medium onions, chopped
½ cup butter or oleo
2 cups unsalted peanuts, chopped
½ teaspoon celery salt
1 teaspoon salt
¼ teaspoon pepper
½ cup chicken broth
6 cups soft stale bread cubes

Cook celery and onions in butter 3 minutes. Add remaining ingredients, mix well. Stuff a 12 pound turkey.

THREE FRUIT STUFFING

2 cups toasted bread cubes
2 medium oranges, sectioned and diced
¼ cup raisins
¼ cup pecans, chopped
½ teaspoon salt
¼ teaspoon nutmeg

Toss ingredients together, cover, let stand 1 hour. Stir. Stuffs one 4 to 5 pound chicken or duckling.

To stuff turkey, use ½ cup toasted slivered almonds to each quart prepared stuffing.

Breads

Breads

BASIC SWEET DOUGH

2 packages dry yeast
¼ cup very warm water
1 cup milk
½ cup sugar
2 teaspoons salt
¼ cup butter or oleo
5½ cups flour
2 eggs, beaten
Butter or oleo, melted

Soften yeast in warm water. Scald milk, add sugar, salt and butter. Cool to lukewarm. Add about 2 cups flour to make thick batter, mix well. Add yeast mixture and eggs, beating well. Add enough of remaining flour to make a soft dough. Turn dough onto lightly floured board, knead til smooth and elastic. Place in greased bowl, brush with melted butter. Cover, let rise in warm place til doubled (about 1½ hours). Punch down. Let rest 10 minutes. Shape into rolls, cover, let rise til doubled (about 1 hour). Bake according to recipes that follow.

CHRISTMAS BRAID

1 recipe Basic Sweet Dough
1 cup raisins
1 cup mixed candied fruits, chopped
½ cup Brazil nuts, chopped
1 egg yolk
1 tablespoon water

Make 3 braids

Add raisins, mixed fruits and Brazil nuts to Basic Sweet Dough recipe with last flour. After dough has risen once, divide dough into 3 parts, then divide each part into thirds. Roll each piece into a 15 inch rope. Place 3 ropes on greased baking sheet. Braid. Repeat with remaining ropes, forming 3 braids. Cover, let rise in warm place til doubled (about 35 minutes). Combine egg yolk and water, brush some over braids. Bake at 350° for 10 minutes. Brush with more egg mixture. Bake 10 more minutes. Cover with foil and continue baking 5 more minutes.

PECAN STICKIES

Makes 18

½ recipe Basic Sweet Dough
¼ cup butter or oleo, melted
½ cup brown sugar
3 tablespoons butter or oleo, melted
6 tablespoons brown sugar
Pecan halves

After dough has risen once, roll dough into 8x18 inch rectangle, spread with ¼ cup melted butter, sprinkle with ½ cup brown sugar. Roll up, beginning at long side, seal edges. Cut into 1 inch slices. Put ½ teaspoon melted butter, 1 teaspoon brown sugar and 4 to 6 pecan halves in each of 18 muffin cups. Add slices of dough. Cover, let rise in warm place til doubled (about 45 minutes). Bake at 350° for 20 minutes.

GRAHAM RAISIN NUT BREAD

4 to 5 cups flour
2 cups whole wheat flour
¼ cup sugar
2 envelopes active dry yeast
1 tablespoon salt
1¾ cups milk
¼ cup butter or oleo
2 eggs
⅓ cup molasses
1 cup raisins
1 cup nuts, chopped

Stir together flours. In large bowl stir together 2 cups of mixed flours, sugar, yeast and salt. In saucepan heat milk and butter over low heat til very warm. Gradually stir into flour-yeast mixture and beat at medium speed of mixer for 2 minutes. Add eggs, molasses and 1 cup flour mixture, beat at high speed 2 minutes. Stir in raisins and nuts. Stir in enough remaining flour mixture to make a soft dough. Turn out onto lightly floured board, knead 8 minutes. Shape into ball and put into greased bowl, turning once to grease top. Cover, let rise 1½ hours. Punch down, cover and let rest 10 minutes. Divide dough in half, roll out each half into 14x9 inch rectangle. Roll from short side, tuck ends under. Place seam side down in 9x5x3 inch pan. Cover, let rise 1½ hours. Bake at 375° for 35 to 40 minutes. Cool in pan 10 minutes. Cool on rack.

RAISIN NUT BREAD

6 to 6½ cups flour, sifted
1 package active dry yeast
2¼ cups milk
½ cup sugar
½ cup shortening
2 teaspoons salt
1 cup raisins
1 cup walnuts, chopped

In bowl combine 3 cups flour and yeast. In saucepan heat together milk, sugar, shortening and salt just til warm, stirring occasionally. Add to dry ingredients. Beat at low speed of mixer for ½ minute. Beat 3 minutes at high speed. Stir in raisins, nuts and enough of remaining flour to make a moderately stiff dough. Turn out onto lightly floured board, knead til smooth. Place in greased bowl, turning once to grease dough. Cover, let rise til doubled (about 1¼ hours). Punch down, divide dough in half. Cover, let rest 10 minutes. Shape into 2 loaves. Place in 2 greased loaf pans. Cover, let rise til doubled (about 1 hour). Bake at 375° for 35 to 40 minutes. Cool on rack.

MISSISSIPPI APPLESAUCE MUFFINS

1 cup butter or oleo, softened
2 cups sugar
2 eggs
2 cups applesauce, unsweetened preferred
3 teaspoons cinnamon
2 teaspoons allspice
1 teaspoon cloves
1 teaspoon salt
2 teaspoons baking soda
4 cups flour
1 cup nuts, chopped
Powdered sugar

Preheat oven to 350°. Cream butter and sugar. Add eggs one at a time, mixing well. Mix in applesauce and spices. Sift together salt, soda and flour. Add to applesauce mixture, beat well. Stir in nuts. Bake in greased miniature muffin tins at 350° for 8 to 10 minutes.

DATE NUT MUFFINS

Makes 36

2 eggs
¾ cup sugar
1 teaspoon vanilla
5 tablespoons flour
⅛ teaspoon salt
¼ teaspoon cinnamon
¼ teaspoon allspice
1 cup pecans, chopped
1 cup dates, chopped

Preheat oven to 325°. Stir eggs, sugar and vanilla. Mix together flour, salt, cinnamon and allspice. Add pecans and dates to flour mixture. Combine flour mixture with egg mixture. Grease miniature muffin tins, fill half full. Bake for 15 minutes.

GINGERBREAD MUFFINS

Makes 24

1 cup sugar
1 cup shortening
1 cup dark molasses
4 eggs, beaten
3½ cups flour
1 teaspoon cinnamon
1 teaspoon ginger
1 teaspoon nutmeg
½ teaspoon salt
1 cup buttermilk
1 teaspoon baking soda
1 teaspoon hot water
1 teaspoon vanilla
1 cup raisins
1 cup pecans

Preheat oven to 375°. Cream sugar and shortening, stir in molasses. Add eggs. Sift flour with cinnamon, ginger, nutmeg and salt. Add flour mixture and buttermilk alternately to sugar mixture. Dissolve soda in hot water, add to batter and beat. Add vanilla. Stir in raisins and nuts. Fill greased muffin tins or cup cake liners in muffin tins half full. Bake for 30 minutes.

PECAN MUFFINS

Makes 18

1 cup brown sugar
⅓ cup flour
Salt
1 cup pecans, chopped
2 eggs
½ teaspoon vanilla

Preheat oven to 350°. Combine dry ingredients and pecans, mix well. Add eggs and vanilla, stir. Fill paper liners in muffin pans ½ full. Bake for 20 to 25 minutes.

RAISIN BRAN MUFFINS

1 cup boiling water
2 cups raisin bran
1 cup unprocessed wheat bran
½ cup plus 1 tablespoon shortening
1½ cups sugar
2 eggs, beaten
2 cups buttermilk
2½ cups whole wheat flour
2½ teaspoons baking soda
1½ teaspoons salt
½ cup pecans, chopped

Preheat oven to 400°. Pour boiling water over brans and shortening. Mix in rest of ingredients in order listed. Store in covered container in refrigerator. Bake as needed in well-greased muffin tins or cupcake liners in muffin tins. Bake for 20 minutes. Batter will keep in refrigerator for 6 weeks.

TROPICAL MUFFINS

Makes 18

2 cups flour, sifted
2 teaspoons baking powder
½ teaspoon baking soda
½ teaspoon salt
½ cup brown sugar
1 egg, well beaten
1 cup sour cream
1 8¾ ounce can crushed pineapple
⅓ cup corn oil
½ cup pecans, chopped

Preheat oven to 400°. Sift together dry ingredients, stir in brown sugar. Combine egg and sour cream. Stir in undrained pineapple, oil and nuts. Add sour cream mixture to dry ingredients all at once. Stir til moistened. Fill paper liners in muffin pans ½ full. Bake for 20 minutes.

CINNAMON NUT BISCUITS

Makes 12

¼ cup sugar
¼ cup walnuts or pecans, chopped
½ teaspoon cinnamon
2 cups Bisquick
½ cup cold water
3 tablespoons butter or oleo, melted

Preheat oven to 400°. Mix sugar, nuts and cinnamon, set aside. Prepare mix according to package directions using the cold water. Shape in ball, put on lightly floured wax paper. Press down and cut into 12 pieces. Shape each into ball, roll in melted butter then in sugar mixture. Arrange in 8 inch round cake pan, pressing down slightly. Bake for 15 minutes. Serve warm.

COUNTRY KUCHEN

- 1 13¾ ounce package hot roll mix
- ½ teaspoon cinnamon
- ½ cup toasted almonds, chopped
- ¼ cup light raisins
- 1 egg, slightly beaten
- ¼ cup honey
- 5 tablespoons butter or oleo, melted and divided

Preheat oven to 350°. Combine hot roll mix, cinnamon, almonds and raisins. Dissolve yeast from mix as package directs, but decrease liquid ⅓ cup. Add egg, honey and 4 tablespoons butter. Blend into dry mixture. Cover bowl, let rise in warm place til doubled. Turn onto floured board and knead. Shape into small round loaf. Place in greased 8 inch round cake pan. Brush top with 1 tablespoon butter. Let rise 30 minutes. Bake for 40 minutes. Cut into wedges to serve.

BRAZIL NUT DO-NUTS

- 3½ cups flour
- 4 teaspoons baking powder
- 1 teaspoon salt
- ¼ teaspoon nutmeg
- ¼ teaspoon cinnamon
- ¾ cup Brazil nuts, sliced
- 1 cup sugar
- 2 eggs, beaten
- 2 tablespoons shortening, melted
- 1 cup milk

Sift together dry ingredients. Add nuts. Add sugar to eggs gradually. Add shortening and dry ingredients to egg mixture alternately with milk, stirring lightly. Dough will be soft. Add more flour if necessary and roll out ¼ inch thick. Cut with floured cutter. Fry in 3 to 4 inches fat at 360° to 375°. Drain on paper towels. Sprinkle with powdered sugar.

PUMPKIN NUT WAFFLES

- 2 cups flour
- 1 tablespoon baking powder
- ¾ teaspoon pumpkin pie spice
- ¼ teaspoon salt
- 3 egg yolks, beaten
- 1¾ cups milk
- ½ cup corn oil
- ½ cup mashed pumpkin, cooked or canned
- 3 egg whites
- ½ cup pecans, chopped

Stir together flour, baking powder, spice and salt. Stir milk, oil and pumpkin into beaten egg yolks. Stir into dry ingredients. Beat egg whites stiff, fold into batter. Stir in nuts. Pour some of batter into hot waffle iron. Bake. Repeat with rest of batter. Serve hot with butter and maple syrup.

QUICK CINNAMON BUNS

2 tablespoons butter or oleo
1 10 ounce can refrigerated biscuits
¼ cup brown sugar
¼ teaspoon cinnamon
¼ cup corn syrup
¼ cup nuts, chopped

Preheat oven to 375°. Melt butter in 8 inch square pan. Snip biscuits into quarters with scissors, place in melted butter. Roll pieces with fork to coat completely. Blend sugar and cinnamon in small saucepan, add corn syrup, cook over low heat stirring constantly til sugar melts. Stir in nuts, drizzle over biscuit pieces. Bake for 15 minutes or til well-browned.

COFFEE DATE NUT LOAF

2⅔ cups biscuit mix
¼ cup sugar
1 tablespoon instant coffee
1 cup water
1 cup dates, chopped
½ cup walnuts, chopped
1 egg, beaten
2 tablespoons corn oil

Preheat oven to 375°. In bowl combine biscuit mix and sugar. Dissolve coffee in water, blend in remaining ingredients. Add to dry ingredients. Stir til moistened. Pour into 9x5x3 inch loaf pan. Bake for 50 to 60 minutes. Cool on rack.

GERMAN COFFEE CAKE

2 cups flour
¾ cup sugar
¼ teaspoon nutmeg
¼ teaspoon cinnamon
1 teaspoon salt
3 eggs
4 teaspoons baking powder
¼ cup shortening
1 cup milk
1 cup apples, chopped
¼ cup nuts, chopped

Preheat oven to 350°. Sift together dry ingredients. Work in shortening with knife. Add eggs and milk, stirring til smooth. Stir in nuts. Pour into greased 8x12 inch pan. Cover with chopped apples, sprinkle with brown sugar. Bake for 30 minutes.

SOUR CREAM COFFEE CAKE

1 cup butter or oleo, softened
1½ cups sugar
1 cup sour cream
2 eggs, well beaten
1 teaspoon vanilla
2 cups flour
1 teaspoon baking powder
¼ teaspoon salt
½ teaspoon soda
1 cup nuts, chopped
1½ teaspoons sugar
2½ teaspoons cinnamon

Glaze:
½ cup powdered sugar
2 tablespoons milk
¼ teaspoon vanilla

Preheat oven to 350°. Cream butter, 1½ cups sugar and sour cream til fluffy. Add eggs and vanilla, beat well. Combine flour, baking powder, salt and soda, add to creamed mixture. Beat well. Combine nuts, 1½ teaspoons sugar and cinnamon. Sprinkle ⅓ of mixture in well-greased 10 inch tube pan. Alternate layers of batter and nut mixture, ending with batter. Bake for 45 minutes. Cool. Combine glaze ingredients, spread on coffee cake.

STRUESEL COFFEE BARS

½ cup butter or oleo, softened
½ cup sugar
1 egg, beaten
1 teaspoon vanilla
1 cup flour, sifted
⅓ cup sugar
1 teaspoon cinnamon
1 cup pecans, chopped

Makes 25 bars
Preheat oven to 350°. Cream butter and ½ cup sugar. Add egg and vanilla, mix well. Add flour, mix well. Spread in well-greased 11x9x1 inch pan. Combine ⅓ cup sugar and cinnamon, sprinkle over batter. Sprinkle nuts over top. Press topping lightly into batter. Bake for 25 minutes. Cut into bars while warm.

QUICK TEA RING

2 3 ounce cream cheese
½ cup sugar
2 tablespoons orange rind
⅓ cup nuts, chopped
2 cups Bisquick
Honey

Preheat oven to 450°. Cream together cream cheese and sugar, stir in orange rind and nuts. Prepare Bisquick as for biscuits. Roll into 12x18 inch oblong. Spread cream cheese mixture on dough, roll up starting at long side. Form ring on cookie sheet. With scissors, make cuts ¾ through ring at intervals, turning each cut section on its side. Bake for 15 minutes. Glaze with honey, bake 5 more minutes.

DANISH DELIGHT

- 1 package refrigerated dinner rolls
- 1½ tablespoons butter or oleo, melted
- ⅓ cup pineapple-apricot preserves
- 2 large bananas, sliced
- 1 tablespoon almonds, sliced
- 4 maraschino cherries, halved

Preheat oven to 375°. Press rolls into bottom of buttered 10 inch pie pan. Stir preserves into melted butter til blended. Put banana slices into butter mixture tossing to coat well. Spoon over rolls. Sprinkle with almonds and cherries. Bake 20 to 25 minutes. Serve warm.

APRICOT NUT BREAD

- 1 1 pound can apricot halves
- ⅓ cup shortening
- ½ cup sugar
- 2 eggs
- 1¾ cups flour, sifted
- 1 teaspoon baking powder
- ½ teaspoon baking soda
- ½ teaspoon salt
- ½ cup walnuts, chopped

Preheat oven to 350°. Drain apricots, reserve liquid. Sieve apricots, add reserved liquid to make 1 cup. Cream shortening and sugar. Add eggs one at a time, beat til fluffy. Stir together dry ingredients, add to creamed mixture alternately with apricot mixture. Stir in nuts. Pour into greased 9x5x3 inch loaf pan. Bake for 50 minutes. Cool on rack. Slice and spread with cream chese to make party sandwiches.

BLUEBERRY NUT BREAD

- 3 cups flour, sifted
- ¾ cup sugar
- 3 teaspoons baking powder
- ¼ teaspoon baking soda
- 1 teaspoon salt
- 3 eggs
- ½ cup milk
- ½ cup butter or oleo, melted
- 1 tablespoon orange rind, grated
- ⅔ cup orange juice
- 1 cup fresh, frozen or canned blueberries, drained
- ½ cup walnuts, chopped

Preheat oven to 350°. Sift together dry ingredients. Beat together eggs, milk, butter, peel and juice. Stir into flour mixture just til moistened. Fold in blueberries and nuts. Pour into greased 9x5x3 inch loaf pan. Bake for 60 minutes. Cool on rack. Wrap in foil and store overnight before cutting.

BOSTON BROWN BREAD

1 cup flour
1 cup whole-wheat flour
1 cup cornmeal
2 teaspoons baking soda
1 teaspoon salt
1½ cups buttermilk
¾ cup molasses
½ cup nuts, chopped
¼ cup raisins (optional)

Stir together flours and cornmeal in large bowl with baking soda and salt. Stir in buttermilk and molasses til well blended. Stir in nuts and raisins. Divide evenly and spoon into 2 greased 1 pound coffee cans. Cover with greased squares of foil and secure with string. Place on rack in large kettle and add boiling water to kettle to come halfway up sides of cans. Cover kettle, steam in gently boiling water 3 hours. Remove cans, uncover and invert bread on wire rack. Serve warm. Delicious with baked beans. Store in airtight wrap. Keeps 1 week at room temperature, 2 weeks in refrigerator, up to 2 months in freezer. Reheat covered in double boiler over simmering water about 30 minutes.

CANADIAN BROWN BREAD

1½ cups dates, chopped
1 teaspoon baking soda
1 cup boiling water
1 egg
1 cup sugar
1 cup nuts, chopped
1½ cups flour
1 teaspoon vanilla
Pinch salt

Preheat oven to 350°. Dissolve soda in water and pour over dates. Add other ingredients and blend. Pour into loaf pan. Bake for 1 hour. Cool on rack.

BRAZILIAN LOAF

1 tablespoon instant coffee
1 cup boiling water
1¼ cups dates, chopped
2¼ cups flour, sifted
2 teaspoons baking powder
½ teaspoon baking soda
½ teaspoon salt
¾ cup brown sugar
1 egg, beaten
1 large apple, pared, cored and shredded
½ cup Brazil nuts, chopped
2 tablespoons butter or oleo, melted

Preheat oven to 350°. Dissolve coffee in boiling water, pour over dates and set aside. Sift together flour, baking powder, soda and salt. Stir in brown sugar. Combine egg, apple, nuts, butter and date mixture. Add to dry ingredients. Stir til moistened. Pour into greased 9x5x3 inch loaf pan. Bake for 60 minutes. Cool on rack.

WHOLE WHEAT BUTTERNUT BREAD

½ cup brown sugar
¾ cup cold water
½ cup molasses
¾ cup milk
1 cup flour, sifted
1 teaspoon salt
2½ teaspoons baking powder
¾ teaspoon baking soda
2 cups whole-wheat flour
¾ cup butternuts, chopped

Preheat oven to 275°. Dissolve sugar in cold water, add molasses and milk. Sift together flour, salt, baking powder and baking soda. Combine with unsifted whole wheat flour. Blend. Add liquid mixture, blend. Stir in butternuts. Pour into greased and floured loaf pan. Shake pan to settle dough. Bake for 2 hours. Cool on rack. Wrap cooled bread in foil, let stand 24 hours before slicing.

BUTTERSCOTCH BREAD

2 eggs
2 cups brown sugar
3 tablespoons butter or oleo, melted
4 cups flour
1 teaspoon soda
1½ teaspoons baking powder
½ teaspoon salt
2 cups buttermilk
1 cup walnuts, chopped

Preheat oven to 350°. Beat eggs, add sugar gradually, add butter. Sift flour with soda, baking powder, and salt, add to egg mixture alternately with buttermilk. Stir in walnuts. Pour into greased loaf pan. Bake for 45 to 60 minutes.

CHERRY NUT BREAD

2 cups flour
1 cup sugar
1½ teaspoons baking powder
1 teaspoon soda
1 teaspoon salt
Juice of 1 orange
1 teaspoon orange peel, grated
2 tablespoons corn oil
1 egg, slightly beaten
1 cup tart red cherries, halved and pitted (or 1 cup canned cherries, thoroughly drained)
1 cup walnuts, chopped

Preheat oven to 350°. Sift together dry ingredients. Add water to orange juice to make ¾ cup. Combine orange juice, peel, oil and egg. Add to dry ingredients, mixing well. Fold in cherries and nuts. Pour into greased 9x5x3 inch loaf pan. Bake for 50 to 55 minutes. Cool on rack.

DATE-NUT BREAD

6 cups flour
6 teaspoons baking powder
1 cup sugar
¼ teaspoon salt
3 eggs, beaten
2 cups milk
1 package dates, chopped
2 cups nuts, chopped

Sift dry ingredients, add eggs and milk to dry ingredients, add dates and nuts. Bake in greased loaf pan at 350° for 40 minutes. Cool on cake rack. Slice thinly, spread with butter or cream cheese and cut into finger sized sandwiches.

CALIFORNIA FIG-NUT LOAF

1½ cups figs, dried or fresh, chopped
½ cup sugar
½ cup honey
1 teaspoon soda
1 cup boiling water
1 teaspoon baking powder
2½ cups flour
1½ teaspoons salt
1 egg, beaten
1 teaspoon vanilla
1 cup walnuts
1 tablespoon orange peel, grated

Preheat oven to 325°. Combine figs, sugar, honey and soda in mixing bowl. Add water, stir, let cool. Sift together dry ingredients. Add remaining ingredients to the cooled pan. Pour into greased 9x5 inch loaf pan. Bake for 1 hour 50 minutes. Cool on rack. Wrap in foil and store overnight before slicing.

GRANDMOTHER'S FRUIT LOAF

1 cup dried apricots, chopped
1½ cups sugar
½ cup shortening
4 eggs
4 cups flour, sifted
2 tablespoons baking powder
1 teaspoon salt
2 cups milk
1 cup pitted prunes, chopped
½ cup nuts, chopped

Preheat oven to 350°. Cover apricots with warm water, let stand 5 minutes. Drain, set aside. In bowl cream sugar and shortening, add eggs and beat til light. Sift together dry ingredients, add alternately to creamed mixture with milk, beating well after each addition. Stir in apricots, prunes and nuts. Pour into 2 greased and floured 9x5x3 inch loaf pans. Bake for 60 minutes. Cool in pans 10 minutes. Cool on racks. Wrap and store overnight before slicing.

GUMDROP BREAD

3 cups flour
3½ teaspoons baking powder
1 teaspoon salt
¾ cup sugar
½ cup nuts, chopped
½ cup raisins
1 cup gumdrops, chopped
2 eggs, beaten
¼ cup shortening, melted
1¼ cups milk
½ teaspoon almond extract

Preheat oven to 350°. Combine dry ingredients, add pecans, raisins and gumdrops. Stir to coat well. Add remaining ingredients, stir only til moistened. Spoon batter into greased loaf pan. Bake for 1 hour. Let stand in pan 5 minutes. Cool on rack. Store 24 hours before slicing.

LEMON NUT BREAD

¾ cup sugar
4 tablespoons butter or oleo, softened
2 eggs
2 teaspoons lemon peel, chopped
2 cups flour
2½ teaspoons baking powder
1 teaspoon salt
¾ cup milk
½ cup walnuts, chopped

Preheat oven to 350°. Cream sugar and butter til fluffy. Add eggs and lemon peel, beat well. Stir together flour, baking powder and salt, add to creamed mixture alternately with milk, beating well after each addition. Stir in nuts. Pour into greased 8x4x2 inch loaf pan. Bake for 50 minutes. Let cool in pan 10 minutes. Cool completely on wire rack. Wrap loaf and store overnight before slicing.

PEANUT BUTTER BREAD

2 cups flour
1 cup sugar
1 teaspoon salt
2 teaspoons baking powder
1 cup crunchy peanut butter
1 egg
1 cup milk

Preheat oven to 350°. Combine flour, sugar, salt and baking powder. Work peanut butter into dry ingredients. Combine egg and milk. Mix into peanut butter mixture, do not beat. Bake in loaf pan for 1 hour.

PEAR LOAF

1 cup sugar
½ cup oil
2 eggs
⅓ cup sour cream
1 teaspoon vanilla
2 cups flour
½ teaspoon salt
1 teaspoon soda
¼ teaspoon cinnamon
¼ teaspoon nutmeg
½ cup nuts, chopped
1 cup fresh pears, peeled and chopped

Preheat oven to 350°. Blend sugar and oil, add eggs one at a time blending well after each. Stir in sour cream, add vanilla. Mix well. Sift flour, soda, salt and spices. Add to the creamed mixture. Add nuts and pears. Pour into greased loaf pan. Bake for 1 hour. Cool 10 minutes in pan. Cool on rack.

PINEAPPLE WALNUT BREAD

- 1½ cups brown sugar
- ½ cup shortening
- 2 eggs
- 4 cups flour
- 2 teaspoons soda
- ¾ teaspoon salt
- 1 6 ounce can frozen orange juice, thawed
- 1 15¼ ounce can crushed pineapple
- 1 cup walnuts, chopped

Preheat oven to 350°. Cream sugar and shortening til fluffy. Add eggs, beat well. Combine flour, soda and salt, add to creamed mixture alternately with orange juice, beating well after each addition. Stir in pineapple, undrained, and nuts. Spoon batter into 2 greased and floured 8½ x 4½ x 2⅝ inch loaf pans. Bake for 50 to 60 minutes.

PISTACHIO BREAD

- 2 cups flour, sifted
- 2½ teaspoons baking powder
- 1 teaspoon salt
- ½ cup shortening
- ¼ teaspoon baking soda
- ⅛ teaspoon saffron, ground
- 2 teaspoons lemon rind, grated
- ¾ cup sugar
- 2 eggs
- ½ cup pistachios, chopped
- ¾ cup water
- 2 tablespoons lemon juice

Preheat oven to 350°. Sift together flour, baking powder and salt. Cream shortening with soda, saffron and lemon rind. Gradually add sugar to shortening mixture. Add eggs one at a time, beating well after each. Stir nuts into creamed mixture. Combine water and lemon juice, add alternately with dry ingredients to creamed mixture, beginning and ending with flour mixture. Pour into greased and floured 9x5x3 inch loaf pan. Bake for 1 hour. Cool in pan 10 minutes. Cool on rack. Wrap in foil, let stand 24 hours before slicing. Delicious spread with cream cheese.

QUICK BANANA NUT BREAD

4 cups biscuit mix
1 cup sugar
½ cup flour, sifted
½ teaspoon baking soda
4 eggs, beaten
1 cup sour cream
4 medium ripe bananas, mashed
1 cup nuts, chopped

Preheat oven to 350°. In bowl combine biscuit mix, sugar, flour and soda thoroughly. Combine eggs and sour cream, stir into dry ingredients with mashed bananas. Stir in nuts. Pour into 2 greased 9x5x3 inch loaf pans. Bake for 50 minutes. Cool in pans 10 minutes. Cool on rack.

STRAWBERRY NUT BREAD

1 cup butter or oleo
1½ cups sugar
1 teaspoon vanilla
¼ teaspoon lemon extract
4 eggs
3 cups flour, sifted
1 teaspoon salt
1 teaspoon cream of tartar
½ teaspoon baking soda
1 cup strawberry jam
½ cup sour cream
1 cup nuts, chopped

Preheat oven to 350°. In bowl cream butter, sugar, vanilla and lemon extract til fluffy. Add eggs, one at a time, beating well after each. Sift together flour, salt, cream of tartar and soda. Combine jam and sour cream. Add jam mixture alternately with dry ingredients to creamed mixture, beating til well combined. Stir in nuts. Pour into 5 greased and floured 4½ x 2¾ x 2¼ inch loaf pans. Bake for 50 minutes. Cool 10 minutes in pan. Cool on racks.

ITALIAN ZUCCHINI BREAD

3 eggs
1 cup oil
2 cups sugar
2 teaspoons vanilla
2 cups zucchini squash, uncooked and grated
3 cups flour
2 teaspoons cinnamon
1 teaspoon salt
½ teaspoon baking powder
1 teaspoon soda
1 cup nuts, chopped
1 cup dates, chopped

Preheat oven to 350°. Beat together eggs, oil, sugar and vanilla. Sift together dry ingredients and add to first mixture. Add squash. Add nuts and dates. Put into greased loaf pan. Bake for 1 hour. Cool on rack.

Cakes and Tortes

Cakes and Tortes

When baking fruit breads and fruit cakes, put pan of water under rack in oven as soon as oven is turned on to preheat. Steam will keep bread and cake from drying out. Add more water as needed.

BANANA CAKE WITH PISTACHIOS

3½ cups flour, sifted
4 teaspoons baking powder
1 teaspoon salt
½ teaspoon baking soda
2 teaspoons cinnamon
1 teaspoon ginger
½ teaspoon mace
1½ cups butter or oleo
1½ cups sugar
4 eggs
4 bananas, mashed
1 cup white raisins
1½ cups pistachios, chopped
2 cups candied pineapple, diced
½ cup candied orange, diced
½ cup lemon peel, diced

Preheat oven to 300°. Set aside ½ cup flour, combine rest of flour, baking powder and salt, sift together. Combine soda with spices and cream into butter. Gradually add sugar. Add eggs one at a time, beating well after each addition. Add flour mixture and mashed bananas alternately. Dredge raisins, nuts, and candied fruits with ½ cup flour. Add to batter, blend well. Pour into greased 10 inch tube pan. Bake for 3½ to 4 hours. Cool in pan. Store in airtight container.

BLACK WALNUT POTATO CAKE

2 cups sugar
¾ cup butter or oleo
4 eggs, separated
2 cups flour
2 teaspoons baking powder
1 teaspoon cinnamon
1 teaspoon nutmeg
¼ teaspoon salt
1 cup cocoa
½ cup sweet milk
1 cup mashed Irish potatoes
1 cup black walnuts, chopped
1 cup raisins
1 teaspoon vanilla

Preheat oven to 325°. Cream butter and sugar, add egg yolks, beat well. Sift together flour, baking powder, cinnamon, nutmeg, cocoa and salt. Dredge raisins in small amount of flour mixture. Add mashed potatoes to creamed mixture. Alternate the flour mixture and milk, beating after each addition. Add vanilla. Add raisins and nuts. Fold in egg whites, beaten stiff. Pour into greased and floured 10 inch tube pan. Bake for 1 hour.

Frosting:
½ stick butter or oleo
2 squares chocolate
2 to 3 cups powdered sugar, sifted

Melt ½ stick butter and chocolate. Add sugar, beating to spreading consistency. Frost cooled cake.

EASY BANANA PUDDING CAKE

- 2 small bananas, mashed
- 1 box yellow cake mix
- 1 3 ounce box banana cream pudding
- 4 eggs
- 1 cup water
- ¼ cup oil
- ½ cup nuts, chopped

Preheat oven to 350°. Combine all ingredients, beat 2 minutes on medium speed. Pour into greased and floured 10 inch tube pan. Bake for 60 minutes. Cool in pan 15 minutes. Cool on rack.

FALL HARVEST CAKE

- 2 cups persimmon pulp
- 2 cups nuts, chopped
- 1 cup raisins
- 1 cup dates, chopped
- 2 cups sugar
- 2 tablespoons oil
- 1 cup milk
- 3 cups flour
- 1 teaspoon salt
- 2 teaspoons cinnamon
- 2 teaspoons baking soda
- ¼ teaspoon cloves

Preheat oven to 325°. Mix together pulp, nuts, raisins and dates. Blend sugar and oil together. Add to dry ingredients. Stir in milk and mix well. Pour in greased and floured 10 inch tube pan. Bake for 1½ hours. Cool in pan. Remove when completely cooled.

KENTUCKY BOURBON CAKE

- 1½ cups butter or oleo, softened
- 2 cups sugar
- 6 eggs
- ½ cup molasses
- 4 cups flour
- 1 heaping teaspoon baking powder
- 2 teaspoons nutmeg
- 1 pound raisins
- 1 cup candied pineapple, chopped
- 1 cup candied cherries, chopped
- 1 cup orange marmalade
- 8 cups pecans, chopped
- 1 cup bourbon
- Apple slices

Preheat oven to 250°. Cream butter and sugar til fluffy, add eggs one at a time beating well after each addition. Add molasses, mixing well. Sift together dry ingredients. Combine fruit, marmalade and nuts, add about 1 cup dry ingredients, mix well. Add remaining dry ingredients to creamed mixture alternating with bourbon, beating well after each addition. Stir in fruit mixture. Pour batter into greased and floured 10 inch tube pan. Cover with greased brown paper. Bake for 2½ to 3 hours or until toothpick inserted in center comes out clean. Cool. Wrap cake in cloth dampened with bourbon, place in airtight container with apple slices. Let cake ripen about one month before cutting.

LEMON NUT CAKE

- 4 sticks butter or oleo
- 2 cups sugar
- 4 cups flour, sift before measuring
- 4 cups pecans, chopped
- 1 pound white raisins
- 1 2 ounce bottle pure lemon extract
- 6 whole eggs
- 1 teaspoon baking powder

Preheat oven to 200°. Cream butter and sugar til fluffy. Dredge nuts and raisins in a little of the flour. Mix nuts, raisins and lemon extract into creamed mixture. Add sifted dry ingredients. Beat eggs well and stir in last. Put into greased 10 inch tube pan. Bake for 2 hours. Cool in pan.

CHOCOLATE-BLACK WALNUT POUND CAKE

2 sticks butter or oleo
½ cup shortening
3 cups sugar
5 eggs
3 cups flour
½ teaspoon baking powder
½ teaspoon salt
5 tablespoons cocoa
1 cup milk
1 teaspoon black walnut flavoring
1 square unsweetened chocolate, melted
½ cup black walnuts, chopped

Preheat oven to 325°. Cream together butter, shortening, and sugar. Beat in eggs one at a time. Sift together dry ingredients 3 times. Add to creamed mixture alternately with milk. Add flavoring and chocolate. Fold in nuts. Pour into greased 10 inch tube pan. Bake for 1 hour 20 minutes. Do not open oven during baking.

HAZELNUT (FILBERT) CAKE

1 package butter cake mix
1 cup hazelnuts, ground
1 12 ounce jar apricot preserves
¼ teaspoon rum or brandy
1 small Cool Whip

Preheat oven to 350°. Prepare cake mix according to directions on package. Stir in nuts. Pour into greased 10 inch tube pan. Bake for 50 minutes. Cool in pan 15 minutes, then cool on rack. In saucepan warm preserves and stir in flavoring. Spoon glaze over cake and let cool. Serve with Cool Whip.

ELEANOR LANE'S COCONUT POUND CAKE

1½ cups shortening
2½ cups sugar
5 eggs
1 cup milk
1½ tablespoons coconut flavoring
3 cups cake flour
1 teaspoon baking powder
¼ teaspoon salt
2 cups coconut, grated

Preheat oven to 325°. Cream shortening and sugar. Add eggs one at a time beating well after each. Add milk and coconut flavoring. Sift together dry ingredients. Add to creamed mixture. Fold in coconut. Pour into 10 inch tube pan. Bake for 1½ hours. Cool on rack.

MACADAMIA POUNDCAKE

2 cups butter or oleo
2 cups sugar
9 eggs
½ teaspoon mace
1 teaspoon vanilla
8 drops rosewater
2 tablespoons kirsch
4 cups cake flour, sifted
½ teaspoon cream of tartar
½ teaspoon salt
1 cup macadamia nuts, chopped fine

Preheat oven to 325°. Cream butter and sugar til fluffy. Beat in eggs one at a time, beating well after each addition. Add mace, vanilla, rosewater and kirsch. Blend. Sift 3¾ cups flour with cream of tartar and salt. Blend into egg mixture. Dredge nuts in rest of flour, stir into batter, blending well. Pour batter into 10 inch greased tube pan. Bake for 1 hour. Cool in pan 5 minutes. Cool on rack.

ORANGE SLICE CAKE

2 cups nuts, chopped
1 8 ounce package dates, chopped
1 pound orange slice candy, chopped
2 cups coconut, flaked
1 cup butter or oleo, melted
4 eggs
1½ cups sugar
2 cups flour
1 teaspoon soda
Salt
½ cup buttermilk

Preheat oven to 300°. Mix together nuts, dates, orange candy and coconut, pour butter over and stir, set aside. Beat eggs and sugar together. Add salt, soda, flour and milk to egg mixture with fruit. Mix together with spoon. Put in greased and floured 10 inch tube pan. Bake for 2 hours. Cool on rack.

GEORGIA PEAR CAKE

2 cups sugar
3 eggs, well beaten
1½ cups oil
3 cups flour
1 teaspoon soda
1 teaspoon salt
1 teaspoon vanilla
2 teaspoons cinnamon
3 cups fresh pears, thinly sliced

Preheat oven to 350°. Blend together sugar, eggs, and oil. Sift together flour, soda and salt, gradually add to sugar mixture. Add vanilla, cinnamon, and pears. Mix well. Pour into greased and floured 10 inch tube pan. Bake for 1 hour.

GEORGIA PECAN CAKE

2 cups butter or oleo, softened
4½ cups flour, sifted
¼ teaspoon salt
1 teaspoon baking powder
6 eggs
1 pound brown sugar
½ cup milk
1 teaspoon vanilla
3 tablespoons instant coffee dissolved in 3 tablespoons hot water
4 cups pecans, chopped

Preheat oven to 325°. Cream together butter and brown sugar. Separate eggs, beat egg yolks well. Add to creamed mixture, beating well. Combine milk, vanilla and coffee, add to creamed mixture alternately with dry ingredients sifted together. Beat egg whites til stiff peaks form. Fold egg whites and nuts into batter. Pour into 10 inch tube pan. Bake for 1½ hours. Cool in pan. Remove from pan and serve plain or with whipped cream.

MAPLE NUT CHIFFON CAKE

2¼ cups cake flour, sifted
¾ cup sugar
3 teaspoons baking powder
1 teaspoon salt
¾ cup brown sugar
½ cup salad oil
5 egg yolks
¾ cup cold water
2 teaspoons maple flavoring
8 egg whites
½ teaspoon cream of tartar
1 cup walnuts, chopped

Preheat oven to 325°. Sift together flour, granulated sugar, baking powder, and salt, stir in brown sugar. Make a well in dry ingredients. In this order add oil, egg yolks, water, and flavoring. Beat til satin smooth. Beat egg whites with cream of tartar til very stiff peaks form. Pour batter in thin stream over entire surface of egg whites, gently folding into egg whites til just blended. Fold in nuts. Bake in ungreased 10 inch tube pan for 55 minutes. Increase oven to 350° and bake 10 to 15 more minutes. Invert pan on wire rack. Allow cake to cool in pan.

SAUSAGE CAKE

- ½ pound pork sausage
- 1¼ cups sugar
- 2 eggs
- 2½ cups flour
- 2 teaspoons baking powder
- ½ teaspoon salt
- ¼ teaspoon baking soda
- 1 teaspoon cinnamon
- ½ teaspoon nutmeg
- ½ teaspoon allspice
- ¼ teaspoon cloves
- 1 cup milk
- 1 cup apple, shredded
- ½ cup pecans, chopped
- 1 container Cool Whip

Preheat oven to 350°. Cream together uncooked sausage and sugar til fluffy, add eggs, beat 5 minutes. Stir together dry ingredients, add to sausage mixture alternating with milk, beat well after each addition. Fold in apple and pecans. Pour into greased 10 inch tube pan. Bake for 50 to 55 minutes. Top slices with Cool Whip.

TEXAS PECAN CAKE

- 2 cups butter or oleo
- 2 cups sugar
- 6 eggs, well beaten
- 1 tablespoon lemon extract
- 4 cups flour, sifted
- 1½ teaspoons baking powder
- 2 cups white raisins
- 4 cups whole pecans

Preheat oven to 275°. Cream butter and sugar til fluffy. Add eggs and lemon extract, blend. Sift together dry ingredients, combine with raisins and pecans, add to creamed mixture. Blend thoroughly. Pour into greased and floured 10 inch tube pan. Bake for 2 hours. Sprinkle with powdered sugar if desired.

SOUTH CAROLINA PECAN CAKE

- 2 sticks butter or oleo
- 2 cups sugar
- 6 eggs, beaten
- 4 cups flour
- 1 teaspoon baking powder
- ¼ teaspoon salt
- ½ pound candied cherries, chopped
- ½ pound candied pineapple, chopped
- 4 cups pecans, chopped
- 2 teaspoons vanilla

Preheat oven to 250°. Cream butter and sugar, add eggs, mix well. Sift 3 cups flour with baking powder and salt. Add to creamed mixture. Mix rest of flour with fruits and nuts. Stir into batter. Add vanilla. Pour into greased and floured 10 inch tube pan. Bake for 3 hours. Cool in pan. Serve plain or with whipped cream.

SOUTHERN PEAR PRESERVES CAKE

1 cup shortening
2½ cups sugar
4 eggs
1 teaspoon vanilla
1 teaspoon cinnamon
1 teaspoon cloves
1 teaspoon allspice
3¼ cups flour
1 teaspoon soda
1 cup buttermilk
1 cup pear preserves
1 cup pecans, chopped

Preheat oven to 325°. Cream shortening and sugar. Add eggs, beat well. Add vanilla. Sift together cinnamon, cloves, allspice and flour. Dissolve soda in buttermilk. Add buttermilk alternately with dry ingredients. Fold in preserves and pecans. Pour into 10 inch tube pan. Bake for 1 hour and 45 minutes.

RUM CAKE

1 cup pecans, chopped
1 package yellow cake mix
1 3¾ ounce package instant vanilla pudding mix
4 eggs
½ cup cold water
½ cup corn oil
½ cup light rum

Preheat oven to 325°. Grease and flour 10 inch tube pan. Sprinkle nuts over bottom of pan. Mix all cake ingredients together. Pour batter over nuts. Bake for 1 hour. Cool. Invert on cake plate. Prick top.

Glaze:
1 stick butter or oleo
¼ cup water
1 cup granulated sugar
½ cup light rum

Melt butter, stir in water and sugar. Boil 5 minutes, stirring constantly. Remove from heat. Stir in rum. Drizzle and smooth glaze evenly over top and sides of cake. Allow cake to absorb glaze. Repeat til glaze is all used.

SPEEDY FRUITCAKE

1 package spice cake mix
1 3¾ ounce package instant lemon pudding mix
⅔ cup apricot nectar
¼ cup apricot brandy
½ cup oil
4 eggs
1 cup raisins
1 cup candied pineapple
1 cup nuts, chopped
1 cup powdered sugar, sifted
2 tablespoons apricot brandy

Preheat oven to 350°. In bowl combine cake mix, pudding mix, apricot nectar, brandy and oil. Beat on medium speed 2 minutes. Add eggs, one at a time beating well after each. Fold in fruit and nuts. Pour into greased and floured 10 inch tube pan. Bake for 50 to 55 minutes. Cool 15 minutes in pan. Cool on rack. Wrap, store in refrigerator 24 hours or more before slicing. Before serving combine rest of apricot brandy and powdered sugar and drizzle over cake.

HERSHEY BAR CAKE

2 sticks butter or oleo
2 cups sugar
4 eggs
2½ cups cake flour
1 cup buttermilk
8 regular milk chocolate Hershey bars
½ teaspoon vanilla
1 cup nuts, chopped

Preheat oven to 350°. Cream butter and sugar til fluffy. Add eggs one at a time beating well after each. Add flour alternately with buttermilk. Melt Hershey bars in a little water. Add to batter. Mix well. Add nuts and vanilla, mix well. Bake in greased and floured angel food cake pan for 1 hour. Cool on rack.

ANN FORD'S SOUR CREAM CAKE

2 tablespoons powdered sugar
1 tablespoon cinnamon
½ cup pecans, chopped
2 eggs
2 sticks butter or oleo
2 cups sugar
2 cups flour
1 teaspoon baking powder
¼ teaspoon salt
½ pint (8 ounces) sour cream

Preheat oven to 375°. Mix together first three ingredients, set aside. Cream together sugar and butter, add eggs. Sift together flour, baking powder, and salt. Slowly add to creamed ingredients, mix well. Slowly fold in sour cream. Do not beat. Pour ½ batter into Bunte pan. Sprinkle ½ first ingredients over batter. Pour in rest of batter and sprinkle with rest of cinnamon mixture. Lower oven to 350°. Bake 1 hour. Cool on rack. When cool sprinkle with powdered sugar.

DUTCH FRESH APPLE CAKE

2 eggs
1 cup corn oil
1 teaspoon vanilla
1½ cups sugar
2 cups flour
1 teaspoon baking soda
1 teaspoon salt
1 teaspoon cinnamon
4 cups tart apples, pared, cored, and chopped
1 cup walnuts, chopped

Powdered Sugar Icing:
1 cup powdered sugar, sifted
2 tablespoons milk
2 teaspoons vanilla

Preheat oven to 350°. In large bowl, beat eggs about 2 minutes, add oil and vanilla, beat til thickened, about 2 more minutes. Gradually beat in sugar. Stir together flour, baking soda, salt and cinnamon. Add to creamed mixture alternately with apples and walnuts, beating well after each addition. Beat at medium speed 3 minutes. Pour into well greased Bunte pan. Bake for 55 to 60 minutes. Cool in pan 10 to 15 minutes. Cool on wire rack. Combine ingredients for icing, beating smooth. Drizzle over cake.

GOLDEN GOURMET CAKE

1 box butter cake mix
1 package instant vanilla pudding mix
½ cup oil
4 eggs
1 cup sour cream
1 stick butter or oleo, melted
1½ cups pecans, chopped
1 cup coconut, grated
½ cup chocolate chips

Preheat oven to 350°. Beat cake mix, pudding mix, oil, eggs, sour cream and butter well. Add pecans, beat til batter turns brown. Add coconut, beat 3 to 4 minutes. Fold in chocolate chips. Pour into ungreased Bundt pan. Bake 1 hour. Cool on rack.

APPLESAUCE CAKE

2½ cups flour, sifted
2 cups sugar
1½ teaspoons salt
1½ teaspoons baking soda
¼ teaspoon baking powder
¾ teaspoon cinnamon
½ teaspoon cloves
½ teaspoon allspice
1 16 ounce can applesauce (1½ cups)
½ cup shortening
½ cup water
2 eggs
1 cup raisins
½ cup nuts, chopped

Preheat oven to 350°. Sift together dry ingredients. Add applesauce, shortening and water, beat 2 minutes. Add eggs, beat 2 more minutes. Stir in raisins and nuts. Pour batter into 2 greased and floured 9x5x3 inch loaf pans. Bake for 55 to 60 minutes.

ARKANSAS SWEET POTATO SPICE CAKE

1¾ cups sugar
1 cup cooked sweet potatoes, mashed
¾ cup shortening, softened
1 teaspoon cinnamon
½ teaspoon nutmeg
½ teaspoon salt
3 eggs, unbeaten
1 teaspoon baking soda
1 cup buttermilk
2 cups flour, sifted
1 cup pecans, chopped
2 tablespoons flour

Preheat oven to 350°. Cream together sugar, potatoes, shortening, spices and salt. Add eggs, beat til blended. Combine baking soda and milk. Add alternately with flour to creamed mixture, beginning and ending with flour. Stir in pecans. Pour into greased and floured 13x9x2 inch pan. Bake for 50 to 60 minutes. Cool on rack.

Yam Topping:
1 cup evaporated milk
1 cup sugar
3 egg yolks
1 stick butter or oleo
1 teaspoon vanilla
1⅓ cups coconut, grated
½ cup sweet potatoes, mashed
1 cup pecans, chopped

Combine milk, sugar, egg yolks, butter and vanilla in saucepan. Cook and stir over medium heat til mixture thickens, about 12 minutes. Add coconut, potatoes and nuts. Beat til cool and thick enough to spread. Spread on cooled cake.

BANANA SPLIT CAKE

2 cups graham cracker crumbs
3 sticks butter or oleo
2 cups powdered sugar
1 egg
Pinch salt
3 bananas, sliced
1 large can crushed pineapple, drained
1 large Cool Whip
⅔ cup nuts, chopped

Press cracker crumbs with 1 stick melted butter in 13x9x2 inch pan, set aside. Beat 2 sticks melted butter, powdered sugar and egg for 15 minutes at high speed. Add salt. Pour into graham cracker crust. Layer bananas and pineapple over custard. Spread with Cool Whip. Sprinkle with nuts. Chill overnight.

BRAZIL NUT DATE CAKE

1½ cups whole blanched Brazil nuts
1 cup pecan halves
1 pound pitted dates
1½ cups maraschino cherries, drained
¾ cup flour
¾ cup sugar
½ teaspoon baking powder
½ teaspoon salt
3 eggs
1 teaspoon vanilla

Preheat oven to 300°. In large bowl, combine nuts, dates and cherries. Thoroughly stir together flour, sugar, baking powder and salt. Beat eggs and vanilla til foamy, stir in flour mixture. Pour over nut mixture, stirring to mix well. Pour into greased and floured 9x5x3 inch loaf pan. Bake for 1 hour 20 minutes. Cool in pan 10 minutes. Cool on rack. Wrap in cheesecloth moistened with brandy, then in foil. Store several days in cool place.

CHOCOLATE CHIP DATE CAKE

1 cup dates, chopped
1 teaspoon soda
1 cup boiling water
1 cup sugar
1 cup butter or oleo
1¾ cups flour
1 tablespoon cocoa
2 eggs
1 teaspoon vanilla
1 cup chocolate chips
½ cup pecans, chopped

Preheat oven to 350°. In bowl mix together dates, soda and boiling water, set aside. Cream sugar and butter. Combine flour, cocoa, eggs and vanilla. Add to creamed mixture. Blend. Add dates, chips and nuts. Blend. Pour into greased and floured 9x12x2 inch pan. Bake for 40 minutes. No frosting needed.

FANTASTIC COCONUT CAKE

1 box white cake mix
1 cup milk
½ cup sugar
1 cup coconut, fresh, canned, or frozen, grated
1 small Cool Whip

Bake cake in oblong pan according to package directions. While cake is cooking simmer milk, sugar, and ¼ cup coconut in saucepan. As soon as cake comes out of oven take fork and dig in cake. Pour milk mixture over it. Cool completely. Spread Cool Whip on top. Sprinkle ¾ cup coconut on top. Refrigerate. Absolutely delicious and so easy!

CRUNCHY FUDGE CAKE

1 package yellow cake mix
1 package fudge frosting mix
½ cup butter or oleo, melted
⅔ cup nuts, chopped
1 cup water
3 eggs

Preheat oven to 350°. In bowl combine 1 cup dry cake mix, ½ cup frosting mix and ⅓ cup butter. Stir til crumbly, add nuts. Press on bottom of greased and floured 13x9x2 inch pan. Blend remaining cake mix, water, and eggs til moistened, beat according to package directions. Pour over mixture in pan. Bake for 40 to 50 minutes. Cool. Frost with rest of frosting mix, use directions on package less 1 tablespoon water.

FRENCH ORANGE CAKE

½ pound dates, chopped
½ cup hot water
1 teaspoon soda
½ cup shortening
1 cup sugar
1 egg
2 cups flour
1 teaspoon baking powder
¼ teaspoon salt
1 cup milk
1 grated orange rind
1 cup pecans, chopped

Topping:
2 cups sugar
Juice of 1 orange

Preheat oven to 350°. Mix soda and water, pour over dates. Set aside. Cream shortening and sugar, add egg, beat well. Add date mixture. Sift together dry ingredients. Add to creamed mixture alternately with milk, beating well after each addition. Add rind and nuts. Pour into greased 9x13x2 inch pan. Bake for 45 minutes. Mix 1 cup sugar and orange juice. Pour over cake while hot. Put back in oven and bake for 10 to 15 minutes or til glazed. Serve from pan.

GERMAN OAT CAKE

1¼ cups boiling water
1 cup quick-cooking rolled oats
½ cup butter or oleo
1 4 ounce bar sweet cooking chocolate, broken
1½ cups flour, sifted
1 cup sugar
1 teaspoon baking soda
½ teaspoon salt
1 cup brown sugar
3 eggs
6 tablespoons butter or oleo
¼ cup light cream
¾ cup brown sugar
½ cup pecans, chopped

Preheat oven to 350°. Pour boiling water over oats, add the ½ cup butter and chocolate, set aside 20 minutes, stir till well combined. In large bowl, sift together the flour, sugar, soda and salt. Stir in 1 cup brown sugar. Add eggs and oatmeal mixture. Beat at low speed til thoroughly combined. Pour into greased and floured 13x9x2 inch pan. Bake for 35 to 40 minutes. In small saucepan combine the remaining butter, brown sugar and cream. Cook and stir til it boils, simmer 2 to 3 minutes. Add nuts. Spread over hot cake. Broil 4 inches from broiler for 1 minute. Serve warm or cool.

JAMAICAN LOAF CAKE

1 ripe banana, mashed
2 eggs
¼ cup rum
1 17 ounce package pound cake mix
½ cup sour cream
⅛ teaspoon nutmeg
3 tablespoons nuts, chopped

Preheat oven to 325°. Blend banana with eggs and rum. Beat into pound cake mix til smooth. Beat in sour cream and nutmeg. Sprinkle greased 9x5x3 inch loaf pan with nuts, pour in cake batter. Bake for 70 to 75 minutes. Cool in pan 10 minutes. Cool on rack.

PEACH FRUITCAKE

2½ cups flour
1 cup brown sugar
1 teaspoon baking soda
1 teaspoon cinnamon
½ teaspoon cloves
1 pound mixed candied fruits, chopped
1 cup nuts, chopped
1 cup raisins
1 16 ounce can sweetened condensed milk
1 cup prepared mincemeat
¼ cup apricot brandy

Preheat oven to 300°. In large bowl stir together flour, sugar, soda, cinnamon and cloves. Stir in fruits, nuts and raisins. Add remaining ingredients, mix well. Pour into 2 greased and floured 8x4x2 inch loaf pans. Bake for 2 hours. Cool completely in pans. Wrap in foil and store in cool place.

PINEAPPLE NUT CAKE

1 cup sugar
1 stick butter or oleo
2 eggs, separated
2 teaspoons baking powder
24 graham crackers, crushed
1 cup milk
1 teaspoon vanilla
1 cup nuts, chopped

Preheat oven to 350°. Cream sugar and butter, add egg yolks, mix well. Mix baking powder with graham crackers. Mix vanilla with milk. Add milk mixture and dry mixture alternately to creamed mixture, beating well after each addition. Add nuts. Fold in beaten egg whites. Pour into greased 9x13x2 inch pan. Bake for 30 minutes.

Topping:
1 cup crushed pineapple
1 cup sugar

Mix crushed pineapple and sugar, cook til thick. Pour over baked cake. Cool. Cut into squares, serve with whipped cream.

SOUTHERN SWEET POTATO CAKE

2/3 cup butter or oleo
2 cups sugar
1 cup cooked sweet potatoes, mashed
4 eggs, separated
2 cups cake flour, sifted
2 heaping teaspoons cocoa
2 teaspoons pumpkin pie spice
1 tablespoon baking powder
1/2 teaspoon baking soda
1/2 teaspoon salt
1 cup pecans, chopped
1/2 pound raisins
1 teaspoon vanilla

Preheat oven to 350°. Sift 1½ cups flour with other dry ingredients 3 times. Dredge raisins and nuts with rest of flour. Cream butter and sugar, add potatoes, then egg yolks, beat well. Add flour and milk alternately, beating well after each addition. Stir in nuts and raisins. Beat egg whites stiff, fold into batter. Pour into 8x4x2 inch pan. Bake for 50 to 55 minutes. Cool on rack.

Frosting:
3 egg whites
1/2 cup sugar
1/2 cup syrup
Chopped nuts

Beat egg whites til stiff. Add sugar and syrup, beat til consistency of whipped cream. Spread on cooled cake. Sprinkle with nuts.

TEXAS CHOCOLATE CAKE

1/2 cup butter or oleo
2 cups sugar
4 ounces bitter chocolate, melted
2 eggs, beaten
2 cups flour, sifted
2 teaspoons baking powder
1 1/2 cups milk
1 cup nuts, chopped
2 teaspoons vanilla

Preheat oven to 350°. Cream butter and sugar, add eggs, mix well. Add chocolate to creamed mixture, blend well. Mix together dry ingredients, add to creamed mixture alternately with milk. Add vanilla and nuts. Pour into 8x12x2 inch pan. Bake for 45 minutes. Cool on rack.

Frosting:
1 stick butter or oleo
3 ounces chocolate
1 box powdered sugar
1 egg, beaten
1 teaspoon lemon juice
1 teaspoon vanilla
1 cup nuts, chopped

Melt butter and chocolate together, blend well. Add sugar, then eggs, blend well. Add flavoring and nuts. Beat to spreading consistency. Spread on cake.

WALNUT CAKE

4 egg yolks
½ cup sugar
2 tablespoons orange juice
1½ tablespoons cognac
1½ cups walnuts, ground
¼ cup dry bread crumbs
1 teaspoon orange peel, grated
½ teaspoon lemon peel, grated
1 teaspoon baking powder
¼ teaspoon cinnamon
⅛ teaspoon cloves
4 egg whites
¼ teaspoon cream of tartar

Preheat oven to 350°. Beat egg yolks til light, gradually add sugar, beating til thick. Stir in orange juice and cognac. Combine walnuts, bread crumbs, orange and lemon peel, baking powder, cinnamon and cloves. Stir in egg yolk mixture. Beat egg whites with cream of tartar til stiff peaks form. Fold gently into nut mixture. Pour into greased and floured 8x8x2 inch pan. Bake for 30 minutes. Cool. Cut into small squares, serve with Cool Whip.

OZARK BLACKBERRY JAM CAKE

3 cups flour, sifted
1 teaspoon soda
¼ teaspoon salt
1 teaspoon allspice
1 teaspoon cloves
1 teaspoon cinnamon
1 teaspoon nutmeg
1 cup pecans, chopped
1 cup watermelon rind preserves, drained and chopped or 1 cup candied citron
1 cup butter or oleo
1½ cups sugar
3 eggs, well beaten
1 cup blackberry jam
1 cup buttermilk

Preheat oven to 350°. Sift together flour, soda, salt and spices. Sift a little flour mixture over nuts and watermelon rind. Cream butter, gradually add sugar, beat til fluffy. Beat in eggs and jam. Add flour mixture alternately with buttermilk, beating well after each addition. Fold in nuts and watermelon rind or citron. Pour into 3 greased and floured 9 inch cake pans. Bake 25 to 30 minutes.

Butter Sugar Icing:
½ cup milk
½ cup butter or oleo
2 tablespoons corn syrup
3 cups sugar
¼ teaspoon soda
¼ cup boiling water
1 teaspoon vanilla

Melt ¼ cup sugar in heavy saucepan, add boiling water, let lumps dissolve. Combine butter, corn syrup, sugar, and soda in large saucepan, add sugar syrup. Cook til soft boil forms when dropped in cold water. Remove from heat, cool. Add vanilla. Beat til spreading consistency. If this gets too hard add a few drops of boiling water. Fill and frost cake generously.

BLACK WALNUT CAKE

½ cup shortening
1 cup sugar
1 teaspoon vanilla
2 cups cake flour, sifted
2 teaspoons baking powder
½ teaspoon salt
⅔ cup milk
4 egg whites
⅓ cup sugar
1 cup black walnuts, chopped
Chopped nuts

Preheat oven to 375°. Cream shortening and sugar til fluffy. Add vanilla. Sift together dry ingredients, add to creamed mixture alternately with milk. Beat egg whites fil foamy, gradually add sugar beating til stiff but not dry. Fold into batter. Add the 1 cup nuts. Pour into 2 greased and floured 8 inch pans. Bake about 25 minutes. Cool on rack.

Frosting:
2½ tablespoons flour
½ cup milk
½ cup butter or oleo
½ cup sugar
Dash salt
½ teaspoon vanilla
½ cup nuts, chopped
1 cup powdered sugar

Blend flour and milk. Cool over low heat to very thick paste, about 20 minutes, stirring constantly. Cool to lukewarm. Cream butter with sugar, add salt. Beat til fluffy. Add flour mixture, beat til creamy. Fold in vanilla and nuts. Spread about ⅓ of this between layers. Beat in powdered sugar into remaining mixture until of spreading consistency. Ice top and sides of cake. Sprinkle nuts on top.

CARROT CAKE

2 cups flour
1 teaspoon baking powder
1 teaspoon baking soda
¼ teaspoon salt
1½ cups corn oil
1 teaspoon cinnamon
2 cups sugar
4 eggs
2 cups raw carrots, grated

Preheat oven to 350°. Sift together dry ingredients. Combine corn oil and sugar, mix well. Add eggs one at a time. Gradually add dry ingredients, mix well. Add carrots, beat. Pour into 2 greased 9 inch cake pans. Bake for 45 minutes. Cool.

Cream Cheese Frosting:
1 stick butter or oleo
1 8 ounce cream cheese
1 pound powdered sugar
2 teaspoons vanilla
1½ cups pecans, chopped

Cream butter and cheese, gradually add sugar. Stir in vanilla and nuts. Ice tops and sides of cake.

CHOCOLATE ALMOND CAKE

2 cups sugar
1 cup butter or oleo
1 teaspoon butter flavoring
4 egg yolks, beaten til thick
2½ cups flour sifted with pinch of salt
¾ cup buttermilk
1 package German sweet chocolate
½ cup boiling water
1 teaspoon soda
¼ cup buttermilk
1 teaspoon vanilla
4 egg whites, beaten stiff

Preheat oven to 350°. Cream butter and sugar til fluffy, add flavoring. Add egg yolks. Add flour and salt alternately with ¾ cup buttermilk. Melt chocolate in boiling water. Dissolve soda in ¼ cup buttermilk. Mix chocolate and buttermilk til smooth. Fold into creamed mixture. Fold in egg whites. Add vanilla. Pour into 3 9 inch greased and floured cake pans. Bake 25 to 30 minutes. Cool.

Toasted Almond Filling:
1 cup almonds, chopped
4 tablespoons butter or oleo
6 tablespoons cream
3 cups powdered sugar
Dash salt
2 teaspoons vanilla
2 drops almond extract

Brown almonds slowly in butter. Remove from heat, add cream, sugar, salt, vanilla and extract. Beat until spreading consistency. Fill layers.

Frosting:
1 box powdered sugar
6 tablespoons cream
1 teaspoon vanilla
3 tablespoons butter or oleo, melted
4 squares unsweetened chocolate
Dash salt

With mixer blend sugar, cream and vanilla. Melt chocolate in butter. Add salt. Add to sugar mixture. Frost top and sides of cake.

FIG NUT CAKE

2 eggs, beaten
2 cups sugar
1 cup buttermilk
1 cup oil
2 cups flour
1 teaspoon cinnamon
1 teaspoon nutmeg
1 teaspoon baking soda
1 teaspoon vanilla
1 teaspoon salt
2 cups pecans, chopped
2 cups fig preserves, drain and cut into small pieces

Preheat oven to 350°. Beat together eggs, sugar, buttermilk and oil. Beat in flour, creaming mixture well. Add spices, soda, vanilla, salt and pecans, mix well. Fold in figs. Pour into greased and floured 10 inch tube pan or bundt pan. Bake for 1 hour. Cool in pan.

Sauce:
½ cup buttermilk
½ cup sugar
1 tablespoon corn syrup
½ cup butter or oleo
¼ cup rum

Bring buttermilk, sugar and syrup to boil, stirring constantly. Remove from heat, add butter, stirring til melted. Add flavoring. Pour over cake while still in pan. Let soak overnight. Turn out onto cake plate.

FIFTH AVENUE CAKE

1 cup butter or oleo
2 cups sugar
1 teaspoon vanilla
3¼ cups flour
3½ teaspoons baking powder
¾ teaspoon salt
1 cup milk
8 egg whites, stiffly beaten

Preheat oven to 375°. Cream butter and sugar til fluffy, add vanilla. Combine dry ingredients, add to creamed mixture alternately with milk, beating well after each addition. Fold in egg whites. Spoon batter into 4 greased and floured 9 inch cake pans. Bake for 20 minutes. Cool in pans 5 minutes. Cool on racks.

Frosting:
8 egg yolks, slightly beaten
1¼ cups sugar
½ cup butter or oleo
1 cup pecans, chopped
1 cup raisins, chopped
1 cup coconut, grated
1 cup candied cherries, chopped
¼ teaspoon salt
⅓ cup bourbon or fruit juice

Blend sugar and butter into eggs. Cook over medium heat, stirring constantly, 5 minutes. Mixture should be almost transparent. Remove from heat and stir in remaining ingredients. Let cool before spreading between layers and on top and sides of cake. Cake is best if stored in airtight container several days before serving.

HICKORY NUT CAKE

3 cups flour, sifted
½ teaspoon salt
2 cups sugar
1 teaspoon vanilla
3 teaspoons baking powder
⅔ cup butter or oleo
1 cup milk
5 egg whites, beaten stiff
1½ cups hickory nuts, chopped

Preheat oven to 350°. Sift together flour, baking powder and salt three times. Cream butter and sugar til fluffy. Add flour mixture alternately with milk. Beat after each addition. Add vanilla, fold in egg whites and nuts. Bake in 3 9 inch greased and floured cake pans for 20 to 30 minutes. Cool on racks.

Frosting:
¼ cup butter or oleo
1 box powdered sugar
1 teaspoon vanilla
4 to 6 tablespoons cream
⅔ cup hickory nuts, chopped

Cream butter, sugar and vanilla til fluffy. Add cream then nuts. Spread between layers and on top and sides of cake.

ITALIAN COCONUT CAKE

2 cups sugar
5 egg yolks
2 sticks butter or oleo
2 cups flour, sifted 3 times
1 teaspoon soda
1 cup buttermilk
2 cups coconut, grated
½ cup pecans, chopped
1 teaspoon vanilla
5 egg whites, beaten stiff

Icing:
1 8 ounce cream cheese, softened
1 stick butter or oleo
1 box powdered sugar
1 teaspoon vanilla

Preheat oven to 350°. Cream together sugar, eggs and butter. Mix flour and soda together. Add to creamed mixture alternately with buttermilk beating well after each addition. Add coconut, pecans and vanilla, mix well. Fold in stiffly beaten egg whites. Pour into 3 greased and floured 10 inch round cake pans. Bake for 25 minutes. Cool on racks. Cream together ingredients for icing. Ice tops and sides of cake.

JAPANESE FRUIT CAKE

1 cup butter or oleo
2 cups sugar
4 eggs
1 teaspoon vanilla
3 cups cake flour
2 teaspoons baking powder
Dash salt
1 cup milk
Add to above for dark layer:
1 teaspoon cinnamon
1 teaspoon allspice
½ teaspoon cloves
1 cup raisins, chopped
1 cup nuts, chopped

Preheat oven to 350°. Cream butter and sugar, add eggs one at a time beating well after each addition. Add vanilla. Sift baking powder and salt into flour. Add flour and milk alternately to creamed mixture. Put ⅔ batter into another bowl and stir in ingredients for dark layers. Pour light layer into 1 10 inch round pan, pour dark layers into 2 10 inch round pans. Bake for 20 to 25 minutes. Cool on racks.

Filling:
Juice of 2 lemons
Rind of 2 lemons, grated
1 medium coconut, grated
2 cups sugar
1 cup boiling water
3 tablespoons cornstarch dissolved in a little water

Put all ingredients except cornstarch into pan and bring to boil. Add cornstarch mixture and cook until thickened. Cool, spread on cooled layers putting light layer in middle.

Icing:
1½ cups sugar
2 egg whites
5 tablespoons water
Pinch cream of tarter
6 large marshmallows

Place all ingredients into top of double boiler. Cook, beating constantly with an electric mixer at high speed for 7 minutes. Remove from heat and add ½ teaspoon vanilla. Frost top and sides of cake.

MILKY WAY CAKE

8 1¾ ounce Milky Way bars
3 sticks butter or oleo
2 cups sugar
4 eggs, well beaten
2½ cups flour
¼ teaspoon baking soda
1¼ cups buttermilk
1 teaspoon vanilla
1 cup pecans, chopped
Powdered sugar

Icing:
2½ cups sugar
1 cup evaporated milk
1 stick butter or oleo
1 cup marshmallow cream
1 6 ounce package chocolate chips
1 cup pecans, chopped

Preheat oven to 325°. Melt Milky Ways with 1 stick butter, cool. Cream 2 sticks butter with sugar. Add eggs and chocolate mixture. Sift together flour and baking soda. Add flour and buttermilk alternately to batter, mixing well. Add vanilla and nuts. Pour into 3 greased and floured 9 inch cake pans. Bake 30 to 45 minutes. Cool on rack. In saucepan combine sugar and milk. Cool to soft ball stage. Remove from heat, add butter, marshmallow cream and chocolate chips. Stir to melt. Add pecans. Fill and ice cake.

MISSISSIPPI MUD

2 sticks butter or oleo
4 tablespoons cocoa
2 cups sugar
4 eggs
2 cups pecans, chopped
2 tablespoons vanilla
1½ cups self-rising flour

Icing:
1 bag marshmallows, cut in half
1 box powdered sugar
4 tablespoons cocoa
4 tablespoons butter or oleo, melted
½ cup evaporated milk

Preheat oven to 350°. Melt butter, add cocoa, mix well. Stir in rest of ingredients in order given. Pour into greased 13x9 inch pan. Bake for 25 minutes. Leave in pan. Immediately place marshmallows cut side down on top of cake. The heat of the cake will begin to melt the marshmallows. Combine rest of icing ingredients and beat until smooth. Pour over top of marshmallows. Let set before cutting. This cake is easy to make and absolutely delicious!

OLD FASHIONED BUTTERNUT CAKE

2¾ cups flour, sifted
¾ teaspoon salt
3½ teaspoons baking powder
½ cup butter or oleo, softened
1 teaspoon vanilla
1½ cups sugar
¼ teaspoon mace
3 eggs
1 cup milk
1 cup butternuts, chopped

Preheat oven to 375°. Set aside ⅛ cup flour, combine rest of flour with salt and baking powder. Sift together. Cream butter, work in vanilla, add sugar gradually, beating til fluffy. Beat in mace. Add eggs one at a time, beating well after each addition. Beat in dry ingredients alternately with milk, beating well after each addition. Begin and end with flour mixture. Dredge nuts with the ⅛ cup flour. Blend into batter. Pour into 2 9 inch greased and floured cake pans. Bake for 25 to 30 minutes. Cool in pans 10 minutes, then cool on racks.

Maple Frosting:
2 cups powdered sugar, sifted
1 tablespoon butter or oleo
¼ teaspoon salt
½ teaspoon vanilla
Maple syrup

Add butter, salt and vanilla to sugar. Blend. Beat in maple syrup til frosting is of spreading consistency. Fill and frost cake.

PISTACHIO SPICE CAKE

1 box devils food cake mix
½ teaspoon cinnamon
¼ teaspoon allspice
¼ teaspoon nutmeg
4 teaspoons instant coffee
1 box fluffy frosting mix
¼ teaspoon almond extract
4 drops green food coloring
2 drops yellow food coloring
½ cup pistachio nuts, chopped

Preheat oven to 350°. Put cake mix in bowl, add spices and coffee. Prepare batter according to directions on box. Pour into 2 8 inch greased and floured cake pans. Bake 35 to 40 minutes. Split each layer in half, making 4 layers. Prepare frosting according to package directions. Add almond extract, food colorings. Fold in nuts. Spread between layers and on top and sides of cake.

WATERMELON RIND CAKE

2¼ cups sugar
¾ cup butter or oleo
4 eggs
3 cups flour
1 teaspoon cinnamon
1 teaspoon nutmeg
½ teaspoon cloves
1 cup pecans, chopped
1 cup buttermilk
1 teaspoon soda
½ teaspoon salt
1 cup watermelon rind preserves, finely chopped

Icing:
2½ cups sugar
¼ cup brown sugar
1 cup cream
1 stick butter or oleo
¼ cup corn syrup

Preheat oven to 350°. Cream butter and sugar til fluffy. Add eggs, one at a time, beating well after each. Sift flour with spices 5 times, add pecans. Mix buttermilk, soda and salt. Combine mixtures, add watermelon preserves. Pour into 10 inch tube pan. Bake for 1 hour. Cool on rack. Combine icing ingredients, cook til mixture reaches 236° on candy thermometer or forms a soft ball when tested in cold water. Ice cake.

SOUR CREAM NUT FILLING

3 egg yolks
1 cup sour cream
½ cup sugar
1 cup walnuts, chopped

Beat egg yolks til thick. Add sour cream, mix well. Add sugar, mix thoroughly. Add chopped walnuts. Boil til thick, stirring constantly. Enough filling for 3 layer cake.

ALMOND TORTE

1 cup toasted almonds, finely grated
½ cup dry bread crumbs
6 eggs, separated
⅛ teaspoon salt
1 cup sugar
½ teaspoon almond extract

Praline Butter Cream:
¼ cup unblanched almonds
⅓ cup water
4 egg yolks, well beaten
1 cup butter or oleo, softened
¼ cup toasted almonds, sliced

Preheat oven to 350°. Combine almonds with bread crumbs, set aside. Beat egg whites and salt til soft peaks form. Gradually beat in sugar til stiff peaks form. Stir almond extract into egg yolks, blend. Fold ¼ of egg white mixture into egg yolks. Pour this over remaining egg whites, sprinkle with almond crumb mixture a few tablespoons at a time, folding in gently but thoroughly. Pour batter into 2 greased 9 inch square cake pans. Bake 30 to 40 minutes. Cool in pans. Cook and stir almonds and ¼ cup sugar in heavy skillet over medium heat til sugar is melted and golden brown. Pour praline mixture on greased cookie sheet. Cool. When hard, break in small pieces, grate in blender, set aside. Combine remaining ¾ cup sugar and water in small saucepan and bring to boil over medium heat (do not stir). Cook til 220° on candy thermometer. Pour in thin stream over yolks, beating constantly. Cool, beating occasionally. Cream butter, gradually beat in egg sugar mixture until smooth and thick. Fold in praline. Put one cake layer on cake plate, fill layers with ¼ praline cream. Save remaining cream to ice top and sides of torte. Chill several hours. Before serving sprinkle with almonds.

HUGUENOT TORTE

4 eggs
3 cups sugar
½ cup flour
5 teaspoons baking powder
½ teaspoon salt
2 cups tart apples, chopped
2 cups pecans or walnuts, chopped
2 teaspoons vanilla
Whipped cream
Chopped nuts

Preheat oven to 325°. Beat eggs til foamy, add sugar. Add flour gradually. Add rest of ingredients in order given except whipped cream and additional nuts. Mix well. Pour into 2 well buttered 8x12 inch pans. Bake for 45 minutes or til crusty and brown. With spatula put one crust on cake plate keeping crusty part up, cover with half the whipped cream and chopped nuts. Put second crust on top and repeat whipped cream and nuts.

LEMON MERINGUE TORTE

3 egg whites
1 teaspoon vanilla
⅛ teaspoon salt
⅛ teaspoon cream of tartar
¾ cup sugar
¼ cup almonds, ground
¼ cup cornstarch

Lemon Cream:
4 egg yolks
½ cup sugar
Peel of 2 lemons, grated
½ cup fresh lemon juice
¼ cup butter or oleo, softened
¼ cup toasted almonds, slivered

Preheat oven to 325°. Beat egg whites, vanilla, salt and cream of tartar til soft peaks form. Gradually beat in ½ cup sugar, beat til stiff. Combine remaining ¼ cup sugar, ground almonds and cornstarch. Sprinkle on meringue and fold in gently. Divide meringue in 3 portions. Grease and flour large cookie sheet. With finger trace 2 7 inch circles on sheet about 2 inches apart, using rim of 7 inches mixing bowl as guide. Spread 2 portions of meringue on the circles. Put third portion into pastry bag with fluted tip. Pipe rosettes around edge of one circle. Bake 25 to 30 minutes or til light brown. Remove with rubber spatula to wire racks, cool. In top of double boiler combine 3 egg yolks, ½ cup sugar, peel and juice. Cook and beat til cream thickens, about 5 minutes. Beat in ¼ cup butter. Cool. Chill, stirring occasionally. Place plain meringue layer on cake plate and spread with half the chilled lemon cream. Top with decorated layer and fill center with remaining cream. Cover loosely with plastic wrap and chill overnight. Just before serving sprinkle top with almonds.

OLD SOUTH TORTE

- 2 tablespoons cake flour
- 2 teaspoons baking powder
- ¼ teaspoon salt
- 3 cups pecans, finely chopped
- 6 eggs, separated
- 1½ cups sugar
- 1 pint whipping cream
- ¼ cup powdered sugar
- 1 teaspoon vanilla

Preheat oven to 350°. Combine flour, baking powder and salt with pecans. Beat egg yolks with 1½ cups sugar til thick. Beat egg whites, fold into nut mixture. Pour into 2 greased and floured 8 inch cake pans. Bake for 20 to 25 minutes. Cool. Whip cream with powdered sugar and vanilla. Spread between layers and on top of cake.

ORANGE TORTE

- 6 eggs, separated
- ⅛ teaspoon salt
- 1 cup sugar
- 1 teaspoon orange peel, grated
- 1 tablespoon orange juice
- 1 cup cake flour, stirred and lightly spooned into measuring cup
- ½ cup orange marmalade
- ½ cup nuts, chopped
- 2 tablespoons brandy

Brandy flavored Whipped Cream:

- 1½ cups cream, whipped
- 2 tablespoons sugar
- 2 tablespoons brandy

Preheat oven to 350°. Beat egg whites and salt til soft peaks form. Gradually beat in sugar til stiff peaks form. Stir orange peel and juice into egg yolks, blend. Fold about ¼ egg white mixture into egg yolks, then pour mixture over rest of egg white mixture. Sprinkle with flour a few tablespoons at a time folding in after each addition. Pour batter into 3 greased 8 inch cake pans. Bake 25 to 30 minutes. Cool on racks. Stir together marmalade, nuts and brandy. Fill layers with filling. Gradually beat 2 tablespoons sugar into whipped cream, beating til stiff. Fold in brandy. Ice top and sides of torte.

WALNUT TORTE

5 egg yolks
1 cup sugar
2 cups walnuts, chopped
1 cup bread crumbs
1 teaspoon baking powder
1 teaspoon vanilla
5 egg whites, beaten stiff
½ pint whipping cream

Nut Filling:
1 cup milk
1 tablespoon sugar
1 teaspoon butter or oleo
½ cup nuts, chopped
½ cup bread crumbs
1 teaspoon vanilla

Preheat oven to 350°. Beat egg yolks and sugar til thick. Add other ingredients, folding in whites last. Spread in 2 9 inch cake pans, buttered and floured. Bake for 25 minutes. Cook milk, sugar, butter, nuts and crumbs together til thick. Add vanilla. Spread between torte layers. Spread whipped cream on top.

Pies

Pies

BRAZIL NUT CRUST

1 cup graham cracker crumbs
½ cup Brazil nuts, ground
3 tablespoons sugar
6 tablespoons butter or oleo, melted

Preheat oven to 375°. Combine ingredients, press into 9 inch pie plate. Bake for 6 to 8 minutes. Cool. Chill before filling.

BUTTER CRUNCH CRUST

½ cup butter or oleo
¼ cup brown sugar
1 cup flour
½ cup pecans, chopped

Preheat oven to 400°. Mix together all ingredients. Spread in oblong pan, bake 15 minutes. Remove from oven, stir immediately. Save ¼ cup for topping. Press rest in bottom and on sides of 9 inch pie pan. Let cool. Chill at least 1 hour before filling with favorite lemon or vanilla pie filling.

MACADAMIA PIE SHELL

1 cup flour
2 tablespoons sugar
½ cup butter or oleo
½ cup macadamia nuts, finely chopped

Preheat oven to 425°. Sift flour and sugar together. Cut in butter til of pebbly consistency. Add macadamia nuts, blend well. Work quickly. Press on bottom and sides of 9 inch pie pan. Bake for 10 minutes. Cool shell. Fill with favorite cream filling.

PECAN MERINGUE SHELL

2 egg whites
⅛ teaspoon cream of tartar
½ cup sugar
½ cup pecans, chopped

Preheat oven to 275°. Beat egg whites and cream of tartar til foamy. Gradually add sugar til stiff peaks form. Fold in pecans. Spread on sides and bottom of buttered 9 inch pie pan. Bake for 1 hour til brown and crisp. Cool. Fill with favorite chocolate cream or chocolate mint pie filling.

NUTCRACKER PIE

3 egg whites
¼ teaspoon cream of tartar
1 cup sugar
10 saltines, coarsely crumbled
1 cup nuts, chopped
1 teaspoon vanilla

Preheat oven to 350°. Beat egg whites til foamy, add cream of tartar, beat til stiff peaks form. Fold in remaining ingredients. Pour into 8″ buttered pie pan. Bake for 20 minutes. Cool. Top with whipped cream. You may substitute 20 to 24 Ritz crackers, finely ground, for the saltines in this recipe.

ALMOND FUDGE PIE

1 cup toasted almonds, chopped
1 4 ounce package chocolate fudge pudding and pie filling
¾ cup corn syrup
¾ cup evaporated milk
1 egg, slightly beaten
½ cup chocolate chips, melted
1 9 inch graham cracker crust
Cool Whip

Preheat oven to 375°. Blend together pie filling mix, corn syrup, milk, eggs and chocolate. Add almonds and pour into unbaked pie crust. Bake for 45 minutes. Cool 4 hours. Garnish with Cool Whip.

ANGEL PIE

- 3 egg whites
- 1 teaspoon vanilla
- 1 cup sugar
- 1 cup graham cracker crumbs
- 1 cup pecans, chopped
- 1 teaspoon baking powder
- ½ cup whipping cream

Preheat oven to 325°. Beat egg whites and vanilla til soft peaks form, gradually add sugar beating til stiff peaks form. Combine crumbs, pecans and baking powder, fold into meringue mixture. Spread evenly in greased and floured 9 inch pie pan. Bake for 20 to 25 minutes. Cool thoroughly. Whip cream. Cut pie in wedges, top with dollop of whipped cream and a maraschino cherry if desired.

APPLE PIE

- 6 medium apples, peeled, cored and sliced
- 1 tablespoon cornstarch
- ½ teaspoon salt
- 3 tablespoons butter or oleo, melted
- 1 teaspoon cinnamon
- 3 tablespoons sugar
- ⅓ cup corn syrup
- ½ cup brown sugar
- 3 tablespoons corn syrup
- ¼ cup nuts, chopped
- 2 tablespoons flour
- 2 tablespoons butter or oleo, softened
- Pastry for 2 crust 9 inch pie

Preheat oven to 425°. Fill pastry shell with apples. Combine cornstarch, salt, butter, cinnamon, sugar and ½ cup corn syrup, pour over apples. Cover with top crust, bake for 30 to 45 minutes. Combine brown sugar, 3 tablespoons corn syrup, nuts, flour and butter. Spread over crust. Put in oven for 10 more minutes.

BLUEBERRY NUT PIE

- 1 can sweetened condensed milk
- Juice of 2 lemons
- 1 cup heavy cream
- 1 cup pecan halves
- 1 16 ounce can blueberries, drained
- 1 graham cracker crust

Mix condensed milk with lemon juice and ½ cup heavy cream, stir in nuts and blueberries. Pour into pie crust. Whip remaining ½ cup heavy cream. Put on top of filling. Refrigerate several hours or overnight.

CARAMEL BANANA PIE

1 can sweetened condensed milk
2 bananas
1 carton Cool Whip
¼ cup nuts, chopped
1 9 inch baked pie shell

Place unopened can of milk into pan of boiling water. Boil for 3 hours, adding hot water to pan if necessary. Spoon milk into baked pie shell. Slice bananas over mixture, cover with Cool Whip. Sprinkle nuts on top. Refrigerate til serving. You can cook several cans of milk at one time and refrigerate them to have ready for quick desserts.

CHOCOLATE MARSHMALLOW PIE

2 cups miniature marshmallows
½ cup semi-sweet chocolate chips
½ cup milk
¼ teaspoon salt
1 cup whipping cream
¼ cup chocolate malted mix
1 teaspoon vanilla
¼ cup nuts, chopped
1 9 inch baked pie shell

In top of double boiler combine marshmallows, chips, milk and salt. Cook, stirring occasionally, until mixture is smooth. Cool until slightly thickened. In bowl combine whipping cream, malted mix and vanilla. Beat til thick. Fold in chocolate mixture and nuts. Put into baked pie shell. Refrigerate 3 hours.

OLDE TYMEY COCONUT PIE

1½ cups sugar
2 eggs
½ teaspoon salt
½ cup butter or oleo, softened
¼ cup flour
½ cup milk
1½ cups coconut, grated and divided
1 9 inch unbaked pie shell

Preheat oven to 325°. Beat together sugar, eggs and salt til lemon colored. Add butter and flour, blend well. Beat in milk, fold in 1 cup coconut. Pour into pie shell. Top with rest of coconut. Bake for 1 hour.

MAKES ITS OWN CRUST COCONUT PIE

2 cups milk
¾ cup sugar
½ cup biscuit mix
4 eggs
¼ cup butter or oleo
1½ teaspoon vanilla
1 cup coconut, grated

Preheat oven to 350°. Combine milk, sugar, biscuit mix, eggs and butter in blender. Cover and blend on low speed for 3 minutes. Pour into greased 9 inch pie pan, let stand for 5 minutes. Sprinkle with coconut. Bake for 40 minutes.

FIG NUT PIE

6 eggs, beaten
1 cup sugar
3 tablespoons lemon juice
3 tablespoons butter or oleo, melted
¼ teaspoon salt
½ teaspoon cinnamon
½ teaspoon nutmeg
1½ cups (9 ounces) dried figs, chopped
1 cup walnuts, chopped
1 9 inch unbaked pie shell

Preheat oven to 375°. Combine eggs, sugar, juice, butter, salt, cinnamon and nutmeg. Stir in figs and nuts. Pour into pie shell. Bake for 40 minutes. Cool.

FUDGE SUNDAE PIE

1 graham cracker crust
1 6 ounce package chocolate chips
16 marshmallows
¼ cup milk
1 quart ice cream, softened
½ pint cream, whipped
¾ cup pecans, chopped

Melt chips, marshmallows and milk in top of double boiler. Let cool. Put ice cream in crust, cover with fudge sauce, whipped cream and pecans. Freeze.

HAWAIIAN NUT PIE

3 eggs, slightly beaten
1 cup corn syrup
2/3 cup sugar
1 1/2 cups salted macadamia nuts, chopped
2 tablespoons butter or oleo, melted
1 teaspoon vanilla
1 9 inch unbaked pie shell

Preheat oven to 325°. Add syrup and sugar to eggs, blend well. Stir in nuts, butter and vanilla. Blend well. Bake for 50 minutes. Cool. Chill. Serve with whipped cream.

JAMAICAN RUM PIE

1 envelope unflavored gelatin
2 tablespoons sugar
1/4 teaspoon salt
1 cup milk
3 egg yolks, slightly beaten
1/4 cup rum
1/2 cup Brazil nuts, chopped
1/3 cup candied cherries, chopped
3 egg whites
1/4 cup sugar
1 Brazil nut crust
1/2 cup whipping cream, whipped

In saucepan combine gelatin, 2 tablespoons sugar and salt. Stir in milk and egg yolks, cook til gelatin is dissolved and mixture thickens. Remove from heat. Stir in rum. Chill til partially set. Fold in nuts and cherries. Beat egg whites til soft peaks form, gradually add remaining sugar, beat til stiff. Fold into mixture. Pile into crust. Chill at least 4 hours. Top with whipped cream. Sprinkle with chopped Brazil nuts if desired.

MACADAMIA PIE

4 eggs
2/3 cup minus 1 tablespoon sugar
1 cup corn syrup
2 tablespoons butter or oleo, melted
1 1/2 cups macadamia nuts, chopped
1 teaspoon vanilla
Cool Whip
1 9 inch unbaked pie shell

Preheat oven to 325°. Beat eggs with sugar, add corn syrup, butter and nuts, blend well. Pour into pie shell. Bake on bottom rack of oven for 50 minutes. Serve with Cool Whip.

MACAROON PIE

4 egg whites
1 cup sugar
1 teaspoon vanilla
1 teaspoon baking powder
¼ teaspoon salt
1 cup graham cracker crumbs
½ cup coconut, grated
½ cup nuts, chopped

Preheat oven to 350°. Beat egg whites til stiff, gradually beat in sugar. Add vanilla. Fold in rest of ingredients, mixed together. Spread in buttered and floured 9 inch pie pan. Bake for 30 minutes. Top with whipped cream if desired.

MAPLE NUT PIE

1 can sweetened condensed milk
½ cup maple syrup
½ cup pecans, chopped
1 8 inch baked pie shell
Whipped cream
½ cup coconut, toasted

In saucepan cook milk and syrup over low heat, stirring constantly, til thick. Cool slightly, add nuts. Pour into pie shell. Top with whipped cream and coconut. Refrigerate.

MILLION DOLLAR PIE

1 can sweetened condensed milk
⅓ cup maraschino cherries
⅓ cup pecans, chopped
⅓ cup crushed pineapple, drained
⅓ cup lemon juice
1 9 inch graham cracker crust
Cool Whip

With mixer, blend milk, cherries, pecans, pineapple and juice til thick. Pour into graham cracker crust. Refrigerate. Top with Cool Whip before serving.

PRALINE DELIGHT PIE

⅓ cup butter or oleo
⅓ cup brown sugar
½ cup pecans, chopped
1 baked 9 inch pie shell
1 5 ounce package vanilla pudding and pie filling
3 cups milk
1 envelope Dream Whip

Preheat oven to 450°. In saucepan melt butter and brown sugar, stir in nuts. Spread in bottom of pie crust. Bake for 5 minutes. Cool. Prepare filling mix with milk as directed on package for pie, cool 5 minutes, stirring occasionally. Remove 1 cup of filling, cover with waxed paper, chill thoroughly. Pour remainder into pie shell, chill. Prepare Dream Whip as directed on package. Fold 1⅓ cups into the 1 cup of chilled pie filling. Spread over filling in pie shell. Chill. Garnish with remaining whipped topping and additional pecans if desired.

PEANUT BUTTER PIE

1 3 ounce cream cheese, softened
¼ cup plus 2 tablespoons peanut butter
1 cup powdered sugar
1 8 ounce Cool Whip
1 9 inch graham cracker pie crust

Beat cream cheese, peanut butter and sugar til fluffy. Fold in ¾ carton Cool Whip, blend well. Put into pie shell. Spread rest of Cool Whip on top. Refrigerate.

FROZEN PEANUT BUTTER PIE

1 cup crunchy peanut butter
1 quart vanilla ice cream, softened
½ cup whipping cream, whipped
1 9 inch graham cracker crust

Mix peanut butter and ice cream. Fold in whipped cream. Pile into prepared crust. Freeze several hours or overnight. Thaw 5 to 10 minutes before serving.

JOE BALL'S PEANUT BUTTER PIE

2/3 cup peanut butter
1 1/2 cups powdered sugar
1 5/8 ounce package instant pie filling
1 9 inch graham cracker crust
Cool Whip

Mix peanut butter with powdered sugar til mealy. Cover pie shell with mixture. Prepare vanilla pie filling according to pie directions on package. Pour over crumb mixture. Pie will be very full. Refrigerate for about 30 minutes. Cover pie with layer of Cool Whip. Refrigerate. Make pie several hours before using. Delicious!

MERINGUE PEANUT BUTTER PIE

1 cup powdered sugar
1/2 cup peanut butter
1/4 cup cornstarch
2/3 cup sugar
1/4 teaspoon salt
2 cups scalded milk
3 egg yolks, beaten
2 tablespoons butter or oleo
1/4 teaspoon vanilla
3 egg whites
1 baked 9 inch pie shell

Preheat oven to 325°. Blend powdered sugar and peanut butter well til it has crumbly appearance. Spread half of mixture on pie shell. In top of double boiler combine cornstarch, sugar and salt. Add scalded milk, mix well. Pour small amount over beaten egg yolks, mix well. Return to milk mixture. Cook til mixture thickens. Add butter and vanilla. Pour into pie shell. Beat 3 egg whites til stiff. Place on top of pie. Sprinkle with rest of peanut butter mixture. Bake til meringue is brown.

PINEAPPLE PARTY PIE

1/2 stick butter or oleo
1 1/2 cups powdered sugar
1/2 pound vanilla wafers, crushed
2 eggs
1 small can crushed pineapple
1/2 pint whipping cream, whipped
1 cup nuts, chopped

Put half vanilla wafer crumbs in 9 inch pie pan. Beat butter and sugar til fluffy. Add eggs, beat til creamy. Pour on top of crumbs. Fold pineapple and nuts into whipped cream. Pour over creamed mixture. Sprinkle rest of crumbs on top. Refrigerate at least 2 hours. May be frozen. Remove from freezer 30 minutes before serving.

NUTTY NOG PUMPKIN PIE

1 cup graham cracker crumbs
½ cup filberts, ground
3 tablespoons sugar
6 tablespoons butter or oleo, melted

Filling:
1 envelope unflavored gelatin
½ cup brown sugar
½ teaspoon salt
½ teaspoon cinnamon
¼ teaspoon ginger
Dash nutmeg
1 cup eggnog
3 egg yolks, slightly beaten
1 cup canned pumpkin
3 egg whites
¼ cup sugar

Preheat oven to 375°. Combine crumbs, nuts, sugar, and butter, press into 9 inch pie pan. Bake for 6 to 8 minutes. Cool thoroughly. In saucepan combine gelatin, brown sugar, salt, cinnamon, ginger and nutmeg. Stir in eggnog, egg yolks and pumpkin. Cook and stir over medium heat til gelatin dissolves and mixture thickens slightly. Remove from heat, chill til partially set. Beat egg whites til soft peaks form. Gradually add remaining sugar, beat til stiff, fold into mixture. Pile into crust. Chill at least 4 hours. Garnish with whipped cream and whole unblanched filberts if desired.

WINNERS CIRCLE PIE

1 unbaked 9 inch pie shell
2 eggs
1 cup sugar
½ cup flour
½ cup butter or oleo, melted
6 ounce package semisweet chocolate chips
1 cup pecans, chopped
1 teaspoon vanilla

Preheat oven to 350°. Beat eggs, add sugar, flour and butter. Stir. Add chips, nuts and vanilla. Pour into pie shell. Bake for 45 minutes. Prepare at least 6 hours before serving. Do Not Refrigerate.

ALABAMA CARAMEL PECAN PIE

1 envelope gelatin
¼ cup water
28 caramels
¾ cup milk
Dash salt
1 cup cream, whipped
½ cup pecans, chopped
1 teaspoon vanilla
1 9 inch baked pie shell

Dissolve gelatin in ¼ cup water. Melt caramels in milk over hot water, add gelatin and salt. Stir until it dissolves. Chill until slightly set. Fold in whipped cream, pecans and vanilla. Fill pie shell. Chill 2 or 3 hours.

CHOCOLATE PECAN PIE

1 cup sugar
⅓ cup cocoa
3 eggs, beaten
1 teaspoon vanilla
¾ cup dark corn syrup
¾ cup evaporated milk
¼ cup flour
½ teaspoon salt
¼ cup butter or oleo, melted
1 cup pecan halves
1 9 inch unbaked pie shell

Preheat oven to 425°. Sift together dry ingredients. Beat liquids together, add dry mixture, blend well. Stir in pecans. Pour into unbaked pie shell. Bake at 425° for 10 minutes. Reduce oven to 350° and bake 40 more minutes. Cool.

CRANBERRY PECAN PIE

3 eggs
1 cup dark corn syrup
⅔ cup sugar
4 tablespoons butter or oleo, melted
Dash salt
1 cup fresh cranberries, chopped
1 unbaked 9 inch pie shell
1 cup pecan halves

Preheat oven to 325°. In bowl mix together eggs, syrup, sugar, butter and salt with fork. Sprinkle cranberries in pastry shell, arrange pecan halves on top. Pour syrup mixture over. Bake for 50 to 55 minutes. Cool.

GINGER SNAP PECAN PIE

3 eggs
1 cup sugar
¾ cup ginger snap crumbs
½ cup pecans, ground

Preheat oven to 325°. Beat eggs for 1 minute, add sugar, beat til thick. Fold in crumbs and pecans. Pour into buttered 9 inch pie pan. Bake for 40 minutes. Cool. Serve with whipped cream.

KENTUCKY BOURBON PECAN PIE

½ cup sugar
1 cup brown sugar
1 tablespoon flour
1 tablespoon bourbon
1 tablespoon plus 1 teaspoon milk
2 eggs, slightly beaten
6 tablespoons butter or oleo, melted
1¼ cups pecans
1 unbaked 9 inch pie shell

Preheat oven to 350°. In bowl mix together all ingredients. Pour into pie shell. Bake for 35 to 40 minutes.

LOUISIANA PIE

¼ cup butter or oleo
½ cup sugar
1 cup brown sugar
Dash salt
3 eggs
1 teaspoon vanilla
2 tablespoons flour
½ cup heavy cream
1 cup pecans, chopped
1 9 inch unbaked pie shell

Preheat oven to 375°. Combine butter, sugars and salt, blend well. Add eggs, one at a time. Stir in vanilla, flour, cream and nuts. Pour into pie shell. Bake 40 to 50 minutes. Cool.

MICROWAVE PECAN PIE

3 tablespoons butter or oleo
3 eggs, slightly beaten
1 cup corn syrup
¼ cup brown sugar
1½ teaspoons flour
1 teaspoon vanilla
1½ cups pecan halves
1 9 inch pie shell in glass pie plate

In medium mixing bowl melt butter on ROAST or medium setting for 1 to 1½ minutes. Stir in eggs, syrup, sugar, flour, vanilla and pecans. Microwave pie shell on ROAST or medium setting 7 to 9 minutes or til brown spots begin to appear in crust. Pour filling into pie shell. Microwave on DEFROST or low setting for 25 to 30 minutes or til knife inserted near center comes out clean. Cool.

PEACH PECAN PIE

¼ cup butter or oleo, softened
¼ cup sugar
2 tablespoons flour
½ cup corn syrup
¼ teaspoon salt
3 eggs
1½ cups fresh peaches, diced
½ cup pecans, chopped
1 unbaked 9 inch pie shell

Nut Crumb Topping:
¼ cup flour
¼ cup brown sugar
2 tablespoons butter or oleo, softened
½ cup pecans, chopped

Preheat oven to 400°. Cream butter, sugar and flour, stir in syrup and salt, mix well. Beat in eggs one at a time til just blended. Add peaches and pecans. Pour into pie shell. Combine ¼ cup flour and brown sugar. Work in butter til crumbly. Add pecans. Sprinkle over pie filling. Bake 35 minutes. Cool. Serve chilled.

SOUTHERN PECAN PIE

3 eggs, slightly beaten
½ cup brown sugar
¼ teaspoon salt
1 cup corn syrup
½ teaspoon vanilla
1 cup pecans, broken
1 unbaked 9 inch pie shell

Preheat oven to 450°. Mix together ingredients. Pour into pie shell. Bake for 10 minutes at 450°. Lower oven to 350° and bake 35 more minutes. Chill. Cover with whipped cream. Very rich, serve in small wedges.

MINIATURE PECAN PIE TREATS

Pastry:
½ cup butter or oleo
1 3 ounce package cream cheese
1¼ cups flour

Filling Pecan:
1 egg, beaten
¾ cup brown sugar
1 tablespoon butter or oleo, melted
½ teaspoon vanilla
½ cup pecans, chopped

Filling Coconut:
1 egg
3½ ounces coconut, grated
⅔ cup sugar

Preheat oven to 350°. Mix pastry ingredients as for pie crust. Pinch off balls, press into miniature muffin tins. Combine ingredients for either filling. Fill shells half full. Bake pecan filled shells for 20 minutes and coconut shells for 12 minutes. Cool. Store in airtight tin. They keep well for 1 week. They freeze well.

APPLE PECAN TARTLETS

Pastry as for Miniature Pecan Pie Treats
1 1 pound 9 ounce can apple pie filling
1 4 ounce package Cheddar cheese, grated
36 Pecan halves

Preheat oven to 400°. Prepare pastry and press into miniature muffin tins. Spoon apple pie filling into shells. Bake for 30 minutes. Remove, sprinkle with cheese. Bake 3 minutes longer. Remove, press pecan half into top of each tart. Remove from pan at once. Cool on rack.

Desserts

Desserts

AMERICAN PLUM PUDDING

2 cups bread crumbs
½ cup milk
2 eggs, beaten
½ cup brown sugar
3 ounces suet, chopped
½ cup flour, sifted
½ teaspoon baking soda
½ teaspoon nutmeg
½ teaspoon cinnamon
¼ teaspoon salt
1 cup pared apple, chopped
1 cup raisins
¼ cup mixed candied fruits and peels
½ cup walnuts, chopped

Foamy sauce:
2 egg whites
1 cup powdered sugar, sifted
2 egg yolks
¼ teaspoon vanilla
½ cup whipping cream

Soak bread in milk, beat smooth. Stir in eggs, brown sugar and suet. Sift together flour, soda, spices and salt. Add fruit and nuts, mix well. Stir in bread mixture. Oil and flour a 1 quart covered mold. Press pudding into mold. Cover with foil, tie with string. Place on rack in deep kettle, add boiling water 1 inch deep. Cover, steam 2 hours or til done, keeping the water boiling. To make sauce beat 2 egg whites to stiff peaks, gradually add 1 cup powdered sugar. Beat 2 egg yolks and vanilla til thick, fold into egg whites. Whip cream to soft peaks, fold into egg mixture. Serve over pudding.

BAKED APPLES ALASKA

4 tart medium apples
½ cup water
½ cup cranberry-orange relish
2 tablespoons walnuts, chopped
1 tablespoon brandy
2 egg whites
¼ teaspoon cream of tartar
¼ teaspoon vanilla
¼ cup brown sugar

Preheat oven to 300°. Core apples, enlarging cavity slightly. Pare about ¼ of the way down. In skillet bring water to boiling. Reduce heat, add apples, simmer covered 10 to 15 minutes. Do not overcook. Combine relish, nuts and brandy. Remove apples from water, drain on paper towels. Pile relish mixture into apple cavities. Cool 10 minutes while making meringue. Beat egg whites with cream of tartar and vanilla til soft peaks form. Gradually add brown sugar, beating to stiff peaks form. Place apples on cookie sheet. Pipe meringue from pastry tube with medium star tip in spiral around apples, starting at base. Cover apple completely. Bake for 20 minutes. Insert piece of cinnamon stick in each.

MINCEMEAT FILLED BAKED APPLES

- 8 large baking apples
- 1 cup prepared brandied mincemeat
- 1 cup water
- 2 tablespoons toasted almonds, slivered
- 2 tablespoons brandy
- 1 cup Cool Whip

Preheat oven to 350°. Core apples, pare strip from top of each. Place in 11x7½x1¾ inch dish. Fill center of apples with mincemeat. Pour water into baking dish around apples. Bake 50 to 60 minutes. Stir nuts and brandy into Cool Whip. Spoon on top of each warm apple to serve.

FRESH CHERRY COBBLER

- 1 cup flour
- 2 tablespoons sugar
- 1½ teaspoons baking powder
- ¼ teaspoon salt
- ¼ cup butter or oleo
- ¼ cup milk
- 1 egg, slightly beaten
- ¼ cup almonds, chopped
- 3 cups fresh tart red cherries, pitted
- 1¼ cups water
- 1 cup sugar
- 2 tablespoons quick-cooking tapioca
- 2 tablespoons butter or oleo
- Few drops almond extract

Preheat oven to 400°. Stir together flour, 2 tablespoons sugar, baking powder and salt. Cut in ¼ cup butter til coarse crumbs. Combine milk and egg. Add all at once to dry ingredients stirring just to moisten. Stir in nuts, set aside. In saucepan combine cherries, water, 1 cup sugar and tapioca. Let stand 5 minutes. Stir in 2 tablespoons butter and extract. Pour into 8x11x1½ inch baking dish. Spoon biscuit topper in 6 mounds over cherries. Bake for 25 to 30 minutes. Serve warm with Cool Whip or ice cream.

CREAM DESSERT SQUARES

16 vanilla caramels
24 large marshmallows
½ cup milk
1 cup toasted pecans, chopped
1 cup whipping cream, whipped
1 cup graham cracker crumbs
4 tablespoons butter or oleo, melted

Melt caramels and marshmallows in milk in top of double boiler, stirring occasionally, about 25 minutes. Remove from heat, cool. Stir in pecans. Fold whipped cream into caramel mixture. Combine cracker crumbs and butter. Reserve ¼ cup crumb mixture. Press rest of crumb mixture into bottom of 10x6x2 inch pan. Pour caramel mixture over, sprinkle with rest of crumbs. Chill several hours or overnight. Cut into squares.

FRESH APPLE SQUARES

2 cups flour
2 cups brown sugar
½ cup butter or oleo
1 cup nuts, chopped
2 teaspoons cinnamon
1 teaspoon soda
½ teaspoon salt
1 cup sour cream
1 teaspoon vanilla
1 egg
2 cups apples, pared, cored and finely chopped

Preheat oven to 350°. In large bowl combine flour, sugar and butter. Cut in butter til crumbly. Stir in nuts. Press ¾ cup flour mixture into ungreased 13x9 inch pan. To rest of flour mixture add remaining ingredients, except apples, blend well. Stir in apples. Spoon evenly over crumbs in pan. Bake for 30 to 40 minutes. Cool. Cut in squares. Top with whipped cream or powdered sugar.

PEANUT BUTTER BANANA DESSERT

6 bananas, sliced
1 tablespoon lemon juice
½ teaspoon cinnamon
½ cup flour
½ cup brown sugar
⅓ cup peanut butter
3 tablespoons butter or oleo

Preheat oven to 375°. Put bananas in 8 inch round baking dish. Add lemon juice and cinnamon, stirring gently to coat bananas. Combine flour and brown sugar, cut in peanut butter and butter til crumbly. Sprinkle over bananas. Bake for 25 minutes. Serve with Cool Whip.

PEACH CRUNCH PARFAIT

1 cup sugar
1 egg, beaten
1 cup walnuts, chopped
1 3¾ ounce package instant vanilla pudding mix
1 cup sour cream
1 cup milk
Lemon juice
1 cup fresh peaches, diced

Preheat oven to 350°. Combine sugar, egg and walnuts. Spread in well-greased 15x10x2 inch pan. Bake for 18 to 20 minutes. Cool. Prepare peaches and sprinkle with lemon juice. Set aside. Coarsely crumble nut mixture. Divide half the crumbs between 6 parfait glasses. Combine pudding mix, sour cream and milk. Beat til well blended. Fold in peaches. Spoon mixture over crumbs in parfait glasses. Top with remaining crumbs. Chill several hours before serving.

PEANUT BUTTER PUDDING SQUARES

1 cup flour
1¼ cups brown sugar
2 teaspoons baking powder
½ teaspoon salt
½ cup milk
⅓ cup peanut butter
2 tablespoons oil
1 teaspoon vanilla
1½ cups hot water

Preheat oven to 350°. Stir together flour, ¾ cup brown sugar, baking powder and salt. Add milk, peanut butter, oil and vanilla. Spread in greased 8x8x2 inch pan. Sprinkle with rest of brown sugar. Gently pour hot water over entire top. Bake for 45 minutes. Serve warm with vanilla ice cream.

IRISH MINT PEARS

1 29 ounce can sliced pears
⅓ cup creme de Menthe
2 envelopes unflavored gelatin
1 cup sour cream
⅓ cup almonds, sliced

Drain pears. reserving syrup, cut into bite size pieces. Marinate in creme de Menthe. In saucepan sprinkle unflavored gelatin over 1 cup reserved syrup. Let stand 1 minute. Stir over medium heat til gelatin is dissolved. Remove from heat. To remaining syrup add enough water to make 1½ cups. Add to gelatin mixture with sour cream. Chill, stirring occasionally til of consistency of unbeaten egg whites. Fold in almonds and pears with creme de Menthe. Pour into 5 cup mold. Chill til firm. Unmold to serve.

RICE PUDDING

2 cups water
½ cup uncooked rice
4 cups milk
⅛ teaspoon salt
1½ teaspoons vanilla
2 tablespoons sugar
2 tablespoons sherry
½ cup whipping cream, whipped
¼ cup almonds, slivered

Raspberry Topping:
¼ cup raspberry jam
2 tablespoons sugar
½ cup water
¼ teaspoon almond extract

Boil water, add rice, cook 5 minutes. Drain. Combine salt and milk, bring to boil, add rice, simmer 5 minutes. Cover, cook 45 minutes, stirring occasionally, til milk is almost absorbed and rice is tender. Stir in sugar, sherry and vanilla. Chill. Just before serving fold whipped cream and almonds into pudding. Put pudding into individual serving cups. In small saucepan combine jam, sugar and water. Boil for 2 minutes. Remove from heat and add ¼ teaspoon almond extract. Serve hot or cold on rice pudding.

SPICED CARROT PUDDING

1½ cups flour
1 teaspoon baking soda
1 teaspoon baking powder
1 teaspoon cinnamon
½ teaspoon ginger
½ cup butter or oleo
1 cup brown sugar
1 egg
1 teaspoon vanilla
⅓ cup apple juice
2 cups carrots, grated
⅓ cup raisins
1 cup nuts, chopped
Melted ice cream or Cool Whip

Stir together flour, baking soda, baking powder, cinnamon and ginger, set aside. In large bowl beat butter, sugar, egg and vanilla til fluffy. Stir in flour mixture alternately with apple juice til well blended. Stir in carrots, raisins and nuts. Pour into 8 greased 6 ounce custard cups. Cover each with greased foil, tie with rubber band. Place on rack in large kettle, add enough boiling water to come halfway up side of cups. Cover, steam 1 hour. Remove cups, remove foil, invert cups. When cool enough to handle, loosen pudding with small spatula and invert on rack. Serve warm with melted ice cream or Cool Whip.

SPECIAL STRAWBERRY SHORTCAKE

½ cup sour cream
⅓ cup shortening
1 egg
½ cup walnuts, chopped
1½ cups flour, sifted
¼ cup sugar
1 teaspoon baking powder
½ teaspoon salt
¼ teaspoon soda
1 quart strawberries, sweetened
1 cup whipping cream, whipped

Preheat oven to 400°. Combine sour cream, shortening and egg, beat til smooth. Add nuts. Sift together dry ingredients. Add to sour cream mixture, stir just til moistened. Drop by ⅓ cup portions onto greased cookie sheet. Bake for 12 to 15 minutes. Split shortcakes, fill and top with strawberries and whipped cream. Makes 6.

UPSIDE DOWN DATE PUDDING DESSERT

1 cup dates, chopped
1 cup boiling water
½ cup sugar
½ cup brown sugar
1 egg
2 tablespoons butter or oleo, melted
1½ cups flour, sifted
½ teaspoon salt
1 teaspoon baking soda
½ teaspoon baking powder
½ cup walnuts, chopped
1½ cups brown sugar
1 tablespoon butter or oleo
1½ cups boiling water
Vanilla ice cream

Preheat oven to 375°. In small bowl pour boiling water over dates, cool. In bowl blend sugars, egg and 2 tablespoons butter. Sift together flour, salt, soda and baking powder. Add to sugar mixture. Stir in nuts and date mixture. Pour into 11x7x1½ inch pan. Combine the 1½ cups brown sugar, 1 tablespoon butter and the 1½ cups boiling water, pour over mixture in pan. Bake for 40 minutes. Cut in squares, invert each on a plate. Serve warm with ice cream.

DESSERT TORTONI

1 cup miniature marshmallows
1/3 cup milk
1 teaspoon instant coffee
1/4 cup toasted almonds, chopped
2 egg whites
1/2 teaspoon vanilla
2 tablespoons sugar
1/2 cup whipping cream, whipped

In top of double boiler melt marshmallows in milk, stir to blend. Stir in coffee, dissolve. Chill til partially set. Stir in nuts. Beat egg whites and vanilla til soft peaks form. Gradually add sugar, beating til stiff peaks form. Fold egg whites and whipped cream into coffee mixture. Spoon in paper baking cups in muffin tins. Freeze until firm. Makes 6 to 8.

PEANUT BUTTER TORTONI

1 cup whipping cream, whipped
1/3 cup creamy peanut butter
1/4 cup sugar
1 teaspoon instant coffee
1 teaspoon vanilla
1 egg white
1 tablespoon sugar
1/2 cup coconut cookie crumbs
1/3 cup peanuts, chopped

Blend together peanut butter, 1/4 cup sugar, instant coffee and vanilla. Beat egg whites til soft peaks form, gradually add the 1 tablespoon sugar til stiff peaks form. Fold into peanut butter mixture. Combine cookie crumbs and peanuts. Fold half into peanut butter mixture. Fold in whipped cream. Fill 6 muffin papers. Sprinkle with rest of crumb mixture. Freeze. Serves 6.

ITALIAN TORTONI

1 quart vanilla ice cream
1/4 cup toasted almonds, chopped
2 tablespoons red maraschino cherries, chopped
2 tablespoons green maraschino cherries, chopped
1 teaspoon rum extract
1 teaspoon vanilla
1/8 teaspoon nutmeg
Whipped cream

Cut ice cream into large chunks, place in cold bowl, stir til smooth. Stir in almonds, cherries, flavorings and nutmeg. Spoon into paper baking cups in muffin tin. Freeze. To serve top each with dollop of whipped cream.

BUTTER PECAN ICE CREAM

2 cups brown sugar
1 cup water
¼ teaspoon salt
4 eggs, beaten
4 tablespoons butter
2 cups milk
1 tablespoon vanilla
2 cups whipping cream, whipped
1 cup toasted pecans, chopped

In top of double boiler combine brown sugar, water and salt. Cook til sugar melts. Add eggs, stir and cook over hot water til thickened. Stir in butter. Cool. Add milk and vanilla. Fold whipped cream into mixture. Stir in pecans. Freeze in ice cream freezer. Makes ½ gallon.

ALMOND FUDGE ICE CREAM

2 large packages chocolate pudding
1 large can evaporated milk
6 eggs, separated
¾ cup sugar
1 10½ ounce package marshmallows
½ cup almonds, toasted

Cook pudding according to directions on package. Stir in milk, beaten egg yolks, sugar and marshmallows. Cook til marshmallows have dissolved. Cool. Beat egg whites til stiff, add almonds, fold into chocolate mixture. Freeze in electric ice cream freezer.

CHESTNUT ICE CREAM

3 cups chestnuts, peeled
1½ cups sugar
1½ cups water
6 egg yolks, well beaten
3 cups cream
½ teaspoon vanilla
½ pound candied fruit, chopped

Boil and rice chestnuts. Cook sugar and water 5 minutes. Add chestnuts, bring to boil. Stir syrup and chestnuts gradually into egg yolks. Stir til cold, add cream, vanilla and fruit. Freeze in ice cream freezer.

COCONUT ICE CREAM

3 eggs
Rind of 1 lemon, grated
1 pint milk
1 cup coconut, grated
1½ cups sugar
Juice of 1 lemon
1 quart cream

Beat together eggs, lemon rind and milk. Put in top of double boiler, beat til mixture begins to thicken, about 2 minutes. Add coconut, set aside. When cool, add sugar, lemon juice and cream. Mix thoroughly, freeze in 2 quart hand freezer. Makes 2 quarts.

FRESH COCONUT ICE CREAM

2 fresh coconuts
Cow's milk
2 cups whipping cream
½ cup sugar

Drain coconut milk and reserve. Grind coconut meat. Place ground meat in bowl with 1 cup reserved coconut milk. Press coconut down so all is covered by milk. Warm slightly and set stand for about 20 minutes. Squeeze as directed for Coconut Milk. Measure squeezed coconut milk, adding cow's milk to make 2 cups altogether. Do not use any of the original reserved liquid. Whip the cream and beat in sugar. Blend with coconut milk mixture. Freeze in ice cream freezer or in trays in freezer. If using refrigerator freezer, freeze then turn into bowl and beat til smooth, then refreeze til firm. Makes 1 quart.

PISTACHIO ICE CREAM

2 tablespoons cornstarch
1 cup sugar
⅛ teaspoon salt
2 cups hot milk
2 eggs, separated
1 quart cream
2 teaspoons vanilla
⅔ cup pistachio nuts, ground
Few drops rosewater
¼ cup sugar
¼ cup cream
½ teaspoon almond extract
Green food coloring

Mix cornstarch, sugar and salt, add milk gradually. Cook in double boiler 10 minutes, stirring constantly. Stir into well-beaten egg yolks gradually. Cook til custard coats spoon. Cool. Beat egg whites stiff, add to custard with flavoring. Mix ground pistachios with few drops of rosewater, add ¼ cup sugar, ¼ cup cream and almond extract, stir to fine paste. Add to custard-egg white mixture. Tint pale green. Freeze in ice cream churn.

TUTTI-FRUTTI ICE CREAM

20 marshmallows
1 cup hot milk
1 cup whipping cream, whipped
¼ cup pecans, chopped
1 teaspoon vanilla
1 small can crushed pineapple, drained
¼ cup maraschino cherries, chopped and drained

Dissolve marshmallows in hot milk, cool. Fold in whipped cream and rest of ingredients. Pour into freezer tray, freeze. When frozen cover with aluminum foil. Serves 4.

Cookies

Cookies

Nuts can be substituted for raisins in cookie recipes.

ALL-AMERICAN PEANUT BUTTER COOKIES

⅔ cup butter or oleo
1 cup brown sugar
1 cup white sugar
1 cup peanut butter
2 eggs
2 cups flour
1½ teaspoons soda
½ teaspoon salt

Preheat oven to 350°. Cream butter and sugar. Mix in eggs and peanut butter. Sift soda and salt with flour, add to sugar mixture. Make into small balls and place on cookie sheet. Press each one with tines of fork. Bake 10 to 20 minutes. Makes 72.

ALMOND FINGERS

1 cup butter or oleo, softened
½ cup powdered sugar
1 egg
1 teaspoon vanilla
2 cups flour, sifted
¼ teaspoon salt
1 cup toasted almonds, chopped
1 6 ounce package semisweet chocolate chips
1 tablespoon shortening
Toasted almonds, chopped

Preheat oven to 325°. Cream butter and sugar til fluffy. Add egg, beat well. Stir in vanilla. Add flour, salt and almonds, mix well. Wrap in wax paper, chill til hard—30 minutes in freezer, several hours in refrigerator. Pinch off tablespoons of dough and shape into 2 inch fingers. Put on cookie sheet. Bake for 17 minutes. Cool on rack. Melt chocolate and shortening over hot water. Dip one end of finger in chocolate, put on waxed paper to dry. Sprinkle with nuts. Makes 48.

ALMOND MACAROONS

- 1 8 ounce can (1 cup) almond paste
- 1 cup sugar
- 2 egg whites

Preheat oven to 350°. In bowl break up almond paste. Mix with ½ cup sugar. Add remaining sugar and egg whites. Beat til stiff. Drop from teaspoon onto well greased cookie sheet. Bake for 15 to 18 minutes. Cool on rack. Makes 36.

ANYTIME FRUITCAKE COOKIES

- 1 cup butter or oleo
- 1½ cups sugar
- 2 eggs
- 2½ cups flour, sifted
- 1 teaspoon baking soda
- 1 teaspoon salt
- 1 teaspoon cinnamon
- 2 pounds dates, chopped
- ½ pound candied cherries, chopped
- ½ pound candied pineapple, chopped
- ½ pound almonds, chopped
- ½ pound Brazil nuts, chopped

Preheat oven to 400°. Cream butter and sugar, beat in eggs. Combine flour, soda, salt and cinnamon, stir into creamed mixture. Stir in fruit and nuts. Drop from teaspoon onto greased cookie sheet. Bake for 10 minutes. Makes 60.

BLACK WALNUT COOKIES

- ½ cup shortening
- ⅓ cup butter or oleo
- ¼ cup powdered sugar
- 1 teaspoon vanilla
- 2 tablespoons thick cream
- 2 cups flour
- 1 teaspoon soda
- 2 cups black walnuts, chopped
- Powdered sugar

Preheat oven to 325°. Cream butter and shortening. Add sugar, cream til fluffy. Stir in vanilla and thick cream. Sift together flour and soda. Add nuts, chopping the nuts in the flour mixture. Add to creamed mixture. Shape into small balls. Place on cookie sheet. Bake for 20 to 30 minutes. Roll in powdered sugar.

BUTTERSCOTCH COOKIES

½ cup butter or oleo, softened
1 cup brown sugar
1 egg
1 teaspoon vanilla
2 cups flour
½ teaspoon baking soda
½ cup walnuts, chopped

Preheat oven to 400°. Cream butter and sugar til fluffy. Add egg and vanilla, beat well. Stir in flour mixed with soda. Add nuts. Pack in 9x5x3 inch loaf pan lined with waxed paper. Chill overnight. Slice about ¼ inch thick, put on ungreased cookie sheets. Bake for 8 minutes. Makes 36.

BUTTER WREATHS

¾ cup butter or oleo, softened
½ cup sugar
1 egg
½ teaspoon vanilla
1¾ cups flour
¼ cup almonds, ground

Preheat oven to 325°. Cream butter and sugar til fluffy. Add egg and vanilla, beat well. Stir in flour and almonds. With star disc in cookie press, force out strips of dough in wreath shape onto ungreased cookie sheet, overlap ends of wreath ½ inch. Bake for 12 minutes. Cool on wire rack. Makes 60.

CASSEROLE COOKIE BALLS

2 eggs
1 cup sugar
1 cup walnuts, chopped
1 cup dates, chopped
1 cup coconut, grated
1 teaspoon vanilla
¼ teaspoon almond extract

Preheat oven to 350°. Beat eggs well, gradually add sugar and beat til fluffy. Stir in rest of ingredients in order given. Pour into ungreased 2 quart casserole. Bake for 30 minutes. While hot, stir well with wooden spoon. Cool. Form into small balls, roll in additional sugar. Makes 36.

CHOCOLATE MACAROONS

- 4 egg whites
- 1½ cups sugar
- 1 cup nuts, chopped
- 1 6 ounce package chocolate chips

Preheat oven to 350°. Beat egg white til stiff but not dry, gradually add sugar, beating til mixture holds shape. Fold in nuts and chocolate chips. Drop from teaspoon onto greased cookie sheet. Bake for 20 minutes. Cool. Makes 48.

CHOCOLATE OATMEAL DROPS

- ½ cup butter or oleo, softened
- ½ cup brown sugar
- ¼ cup sugar
- 1 egg
- 1 teaspoon vanilla
- ⅔ cup whole-wheat flour
- ¼ teaspoon salt
- ½ teaspoon baking soda
- 1 cup quick cooking rolled oats
- 1 cup semisweet chocolate chips
- ½ cup nuts, chopped
- ½ cup raisins

Preheat oven to 375°. Cream butter and sugars, add egg and vanilla, beat til fluffy. Mix flour with salt and soda. Stir into creamed mixture, blending well. Add remaining ingredients. Drop by teaspoonfuls onto greased cookie sheet. Bake for 10 to 12 minutes. Cool on rack. Makes 36.

COCONUT CRUNCHIES

- 1 cup shortening
- 1 cup brown sugar
- ½ cup granulated sugar
- 2 eggs
- 2 tablespoons milk
- 1 teaspoon vanilla
- 2 cups flour, sifted
- 1 teaspoon baking soda
- 1 teaspoon salt
- ½ cup walnuts, chopped
- 3 1⅝ ounce chocolate coconut candy bars, chilled and diced

Preheat oven to 375°. Cream shortening and sugar. Add eggs, milk and vanilla, beat til fluffy. Sift dry ingredients, blend into creamed mixture. Stir in nuts, fold in candy. Drop by tablespoons 2 inches apart on ungreased cookie sheet. Bake for 10 to 12 minutes. Cool. Makes 48.

COCONUT LEMON CRISPS

½ cup butter or oleo, softened
Sugar
1 egg, separated
Juice and grated rind of 1 lemon
⅓ cup coconut, grated
1 cup flour
½ teaspoon baking soda
1 teaspoon cream of tartar
Candied fruit
Pecan halves

Preheat oven to 350°. Cream butter and sugar, beat in egg yolk, juice and rind. Add coconut. Sift together dry ingredients, add to creamed mixture. Drop by small teaspoonful onto greased cookie sheet. Brush lightly with unbeaten egg white, sprinkle with small amount of sugar. Decorate tops with small piece candied fruit or nut half. Bake for 12 to 15 minutes. Makes 84.

COCONUT MACAROONS

⅔ cup sweetened condensed milk
3 cups coconut, grated
1 teaspoon vanilla

Preheat oven to 350°. Mix together all ingredients. Drop by teaspoonful onto greased cookie sheet, about 1 inch apart. Bake for 8 to 10 minutes. Cool on rack.

DATE COOKIES

1 cup sugar
1 cup brown sugar
1 cup butter or oleo
3 eggs, well beaten
3 cups flour
1 teaspoon salt
1 teaspoon soda
1 teaspoon baking powder
2 cups dates, chopped
2 cups nuts, chopped

Preheat oven to 300°. Cream sugar and butter til fluffy. Add eggs, beat well. Combine dry ingredients, add to creamed mixture, mix well. Stir in dates and nuts. Roll dough into walnut size balls, flatten. Place on greased cookie sheets. Bake for 15 minutes. Makes 48.

DATE NUT COOKIES

½ cup butter or oleo, softened
⅓ cup brown sugar
⅓ cup sugar
1 egg
½ teaspoon vanilla
1 teaspoon warm water
1 cup plus 2 tablespoons flour
¼ teaspoon baking soda
¼ teaspoon salt
½ cup pecans, chopped
½ cup dates, chopped

Preheat oven to 375°. Cream butter and sugars, add egg, beat til light. Add vanilla and water. Gradually stir in flour mixed with soda and salt. Stir in nuts and dates. Drop by teaspoonfuls on ungreased cookie sheet about 2 inches apart. Bake for 10 minutes. Cool on rack. Makes 26.

FILBERT FANCIES

1 cup unblanched toasted filberts, chopped
2 cups powdered sugar, sifted
2 tablespoons butter or oleo, softened
1 teaspoon vanilla
Dash salt
1 egg, beaten
2 squares unsweetened chocolate, melted and cooled
4 cups miniature marshmallows
1 cup coconut, grated

Beat powdered sugar, butter, vanilla and salt into egg til fluffy. Add cooled chocolate. Fold into marshmallows and nuts. Drop by teaspoonful into bowl of coconut, roll evenly to coat. Place on wax paper on cookie sheet. Let stand til set. Makes 48.

FRUITCAKE COOKIES

- 1 pound candied pineapple, diced
- ½ pound candied red cherries, chopped
- ½ pound candied green cherries, chopped
- 4 cups nuts, chopped
- 3½ cups flour, divided
- ½ cup butter or oleo, softened
- 1 cup brown sugar
- 4 eggs, separated
- 3 teaspoons soda
- 3 tablespoons milk
- ¼ cup brandy
- 1 teaspoon cinnamon
- 1 teaspoon nutmeg

Preheat oven to 325°. In bowl mix 1 cup flour with fruit and nuts. Cream butter and brown sugar til fluffy. Blend in egg yolks. Dissolve soda in milk, stir into creamed mixture. Add brandy, spices and rest of flour, mix well. Beat egg whites til stiff but not dry, fold into batter. Stir in fruit mixture. Drop by teaspoon onto greased cookie sheets. Bake for 15 to 18 minutes. Makes 10 dozen.

FRUIT NUT ROCKS

- 1 cup butter or oleo, softened
- 1 cup brown sugar
- 2 eggs, beaten
- 1 teaspoon vanilla
- 3 cups flour
- ½ teaspoon soda
- ¼ teaspoon salt
- ⅓ cup hot water
- 1 cup dates, chopped
- 1 cup raisins
- 1 cup nuts, chopped

Preheat oven to 400°. Cream butter, add sugar, eggs and vanilla, beat well. Add dry ingredients, add water, mix well. Stir in fruits and nuts. Drop by teaspoonful onto cookie sheet. Bake for 10 to 12 minutes. Makes 48.

GRANDMA'S OATMEAL COOKIES

1 cup raisins
1 cup water
¾ cup shortening
1½ cups sugar
2 eggs
1 teaspoon vanilla
2½ cups flour
1 teaspoon soda
1 teaspoon salt
1 teaspoon cinnamon
½ teaspoon baking powder
½ teaspoon cloves
2 cups oats
½ cup nuts, chopped

Preheat oven to 400°. Simmer raisins and water over medium heat til raisins are plump. Drain, reserving liquid. Add water to liquid to make ½ cup. Mix shortening, sugar, eggs and vanilla. Stir in reserved liquid. Blend in remaining ingredients. Drop by teaspoonfuls 2 inches apart on ungreased cookie sheet. Bake for 8 to 10 minutes. Makes 72.

JAM THUMBPRINT COOKIES

¾ cup butter or oleo
½ cup sugar
2 eggs
1½ teaspoons vanilla
2 cups flour
1½ teaspoons baking powder
¼ teaspoon salt
½ cup red raspberry jam
⅓ cup filberts, chopped
1 teaspoon orange peel, grated
2 egg whites
¼ teaspoon cream of tartar
½ cup sugar

Preheat oven to 350°. Cream butter and sugar til fluffy. Add eggs and vanilla, beat well. Stir together dry ingredients, stir into creamed mixture. Chill 1 hour. Divide dough into 48 balls. Place 2 inches apart on greased cookie sheet. Moisten finger, make indention in each cookie. Combine jam, nuts and peel. Place ½ teaspoonful in center of each cookie. Beat egg whites with cream of tartar til soft peaks form. Gradually add the second sugar, beat to stiff peaks. Pipe wreath of meringue onto each cookie. Bake for 10 to 13 minutes. Makes 48.

LACE COOKIES

2 cups quick oatmeal
3 tablespoons flour
¼ teaspoon baking powder
2 cups sugar
2 eggs, beaten
1 cup butter or oleo, melted
1 teaspoon vanilla
1 teaspoon lemon extract
¼ teaspoon almond extract
1 cup pecans, chopped

Preheat oven to 350°. Combine oatmeal, flour, baking powder and sugar. Combine eggs and butter, mix with oatmeal mixture. Add rest of ingredients. Cover cookie sheet with foil, drop batter by ½ teaspoonful on foil. Bake for 9 to 10 minutes. Cool. Slide knife under cookies to remove from foil.

MAPLE PRALINE COOKIES

⅔ cup brown sugar
⅔ cup shortening
1 egg
½ cup milk
½ teaspoon maple flavoring
2 cups flour, sifted
¼ teaspoon baking soda
¼ teaspoon salt
2 cups Rice Krispies
Pecan halves

Preheat oven to 375°. In bowl cream sugar and shortening til fluffy, beat in egg. Stir in milk and flavoring (mixture will look curdled). Sift together dry ingredients, add to creamed mixture, mix well. Stir in Rice Crispies. Drop from teaspoon 2 inches apart onto greased cookie sheet. Flatten with bottom of glass dipped into sugar. Top each with a pecan half. Bake for 8 to 10 minutes. Makes 48.

MERINGUE HEARTS

3 egg whites
2½ cups powdered sugar, sifted
½ teaspoon lemon peel, grated
½ teaspoon almond extract
2 cups pecans, chopped
½ teaspoon cinnamon

Preheat oven to 275°. Beat egg whites til soft peaks form, gradually add sugar, beat mixture til stiff, about 15 minutes. Stir in lemon peel and extract. Divide meringue into two parts. Stir nuts and cinnamon into one half. Using 2 teaspoons cinnamon-nut meringue for each cookie, drop mixture onto greased cookie sheet. Shape into hearts with spoon. Spread 1 teaspoon plain meringue over nut hearts, following same outline. Bake for 25 to 30 minutes. Cool on wire rack. Makes 60.

NORMA'S NUTTY FINGERS

2 cups flour
2 sticks butter or oleo, softened
1½ cups nuts, chopped
4 tablespoons sugar
2 teaspoons vanilla
Powdered sugar

Preheat oven to 350°. With fingers work together all ingredients except powdered sugar til you can pinch off dough and roll in hand into small fingers or balls. Put on ungreased cookie sheet. Bake for 20 minutes. Immediately roll in powdered sugar. Let cool. Roll in powdered sugar again. These keep for weeks in airtight tin. Makes 72.

NUT EDGED COOKIES

½ cup butter or oleo
⅔ cup sugar
1 egg yolk
2 tablespoons milk
1 teaspoon vanilla
1½ cups flour, sifted
2 teaspoons baking powder
½ teaspoon salt
½ cup toasted almonds, chopped
3 tablespoons sugar
1 egg white, slightly beaten

Preheat oven to 400°. Cream butter and sugar, add egg yolk, milk and vanilla, beat well. Sift together dry ingredients, gradually add to creamed mixture, beating well. On wax paper shape dough into 12x1½ inch roll. Chill 1 hour. Combine almonds and 3 tablespoons sugar. Brush chilled dough with egg white, roll in almond mixture, press nuts in firmly. Cut into ¼ inch slices. Place on greased cookie sheet. Bake for 7 to 10 minutes. Makes 48.

NUT MACAROONS

3 egg whites
1 cup sugar
½ teaspoon cream of tartar
2 cups pecans, ground
½ teaspoon vanilla

Preheat oven to 300°. Beat egg whites til stiff, add sugar and cream of tartar gradually. Fold in nuts and vanilla. Drop from teaspoon onto greased and floured cookie sheet. Bake for 20 minutes. Makes 50.

PECAN MERINGUE COOKIES

1 egg white
1 cup brown sugar
¼ teaspoon salt
1 tablespoon flour
1 cup pecans, chopped
Pecan halves

Preheat oven to 300°. In small bowl beat egg white til stiff. Slowly beat in sugar, salt and flour. Stir in chopped pecans. Drop by teaspoonful onto greased cookie sheet. Place pecan half on each. Bake for 15 minutes.

PEANUT BRITTLE COOKIES

1 stick piecrust mix
¾ cup brown sugar
1 egg, slightly beaten
½ teaspoon vanilla
¾ cup peanuts, chopped

Preheat oven to 350°. Mix piecrust mix according to package directions, do not roll out. Cut in brown sugar til mixture resembles crumbs. Add egg, vanilla and ¼ cup of peanuts, mix well. Spread mixture on greased and floured cookie sheet to 12x12 inch square. Press rest of peanuts into dough. Bake for 15 to 20 minutes. Loosen edges as soon as removed from oven. Cool on sheet, cut into 2 inch squares. Makes 36.

PUMPKIN COOKIES

2 cups sugar
2 cups shortening
1 16 ounce can pumpkin
2 eggs
2 teaspoons vanilla
4 cups flour, sifted
2 teaspoons baking powder
1 teaspoon baking soda
1 teaspoon salt
2 teaspoons cinnamon
1 teaspoon nutmeg
½ teaspoon allspice
2 cups raisins
1 cup nuts, chopped

Preheat oven to 350°. In bowl cream sugar and shortening til fluffy. Add pumpkin, eggs and vanilla, beat well. Sift together dry ingredients. Add to creamed mixture, mix well. Stir in raisins and nuts. Drop dough from teaspoon onto greased cookie sheet 2 inches apart. Bake for 12 to 15 minutes. Cool. Frost with vanilla frosting, if desired. Makes 84.

QUICK PEANUT BUTTER COOKIES

1 cup crunchy peanut butter
½ cup shortening
1 2 layer size yellow cake mix
2 eggs
2 tablespoons water

Preheat oven to 350°. Cut peanut butter and shortening into dry cake mix using low speed on electric mixer. Add eggs and water, mix well to form dough. Using 1 tablespoon dough for each cookie, shape into 1½ inch balls. Place on ungreased cookie sheet and flatten each with fork. Bake for 15 minutes. Cool thoroughly. Makes 54.

SWEDISH SAND COOKIES

¾ cup powdered sugar
½ cup butter or oleo, softened
1 egg yolk
1 cup flour
⅓ cup almonds, chopped
⅛ teaspoon cardamon

Preheat oven to 350°. Cream sugar and butter til fluffy. Beat in egg yolk. Stir together remaining ingredients, blend into creamed mixture. Pinch off small balls and press in center of tiny foil cup. Press dough down with thumb very thinly over bottom and up sides. Place cups on cookie sheet. Bake for 12 to 15 minutes. Cool. Remove from cups, fill with jam or jelly. Makes 30.

SWISS TREATS

1 cup whole unblanched almonds
1 cup filberts
2 tablespoons candied citron
2 tablespoons candied orange peel
½ cup cake flour, sifted
1 teaspoon cinnamon
¼ teaspoon cloves
2 egg whites
1 cup sugar
½ cup apricot preserves
Whole almonds
1 egg white
1 tablespoon water

Preheat oven to 350°. In blender grind nuts and candied fruit. In bowl stir together ground mixture and dry ingredients. Set aside. In small bowl beat egg whites til foamy, gradually beat in sugar til soft peaks form. Fold into nut mixture, stir in apricot preserves. Spoon by rounded tablespoons onto greased cookie sheet, spread into 2 one half inch circles. Arrange 3 whole almonds on top of each cookie. Let stand uncovered at room temperature for 2 hours to dry. Bake for 20 to 22 minutes. Combine remaining egg white and water, brush over hot cookies. Cool on rack. Makes 24.

SYRUP COOKIES

1 cup butter or oleo
⅔ cup sugar
½ cup dark corn syrup
⅓ cup milk
3½ cups flour
½ teaspoon cream of tartar
½ teaspoon white pepper
¼ teaspoon ginger
½ cup almonds, halved

Preheat oven to 325°. In saucepan combine butter, sugar and corn syrup, bring to boil. Cool to room temperature. Blend in milk. Stir together dry ingredients, stir in syrup mixture. Divide dough in half, wrap in waxed paper, chill 2 hours at least. On floured board, roll half dough at a time to ¼ inch thickness. Trim to 12 inch square. Cut into diamond shapes. Place on ungreased cookie sheet. Press one almond half in center of each cookie. Bake for 15 to 17 minutes. Cool. Makes 96 cookies.

BROWNIES

4 1 ounce squares unsweetened chocolate
¾ cup butter
4 eggs
2 cups sugar
1 cup flour, sifted
1 teaspoon vanilla
1 cup pecans, chopped

Preheat oven to 325°. Melt chocolate and butter together, cool. Beat eggs, add sugar, flour, chocolate, mixture, vanilla and pecans. Pour into 2 greased and floured 7x7 inch pans. Bake for 30 minutes. Do not overcook. Makes 12.

APPLE BROWNIES

⅔ cup butter or oleo
2 cups brown sugar
1 cup applesauce
2 eggs
1 tablespoon orange peel, grated
2 teaspoons vanilla
2 cups flour, sifted
2 teaspoons baking powder
1 teaspoon salt
½ teaspoon baking soda
1 cup walnuts, chopped

Preheat oven to 350°. In saucepan melt butter, remove from heat. Add brown sugar, stir til blended, cool. Beat in applesauce, eggs, orange peel and vanilla. Sift together dry ingredients, stir into applesauce mixture, stir in nuts. Spread in greased 15x10x1 inch pan. Bake for 25 to 30 minutes. Makes 48.

COCONUT BROWNIES

1 cup butter or oleo
1¼ cups sugar
3 eggs
1 cup flour
3 tablespoons cocoa
¼ teaspoon salt
1 cup nuts, chopped
2½ cups coconut, grated
1 can sweetened condensed milk

Frosting:
⅓ cup scalded milk
¼ cup butter or oleo
1 6 ounce package chocolate chips
2¼ cups powdered sugar
1 teaspoon vanilla

Preheat oven to 350°. Cream butter and sugar. Add eggs, flour, cocoa, salt and nuts, mix well. Pour into greased 10x15 inch pan. Bake for 20 minutes. Mix coconut with condensed milk. Spread on hot cake as soon as taken from oven. Bake for 15 minutes. Cool at least 5 minutes. Add butter and chocolate chips to scalded milk, stir til melted. Add sugar, mix. Add vanilla. Frost cake. Cut into squares to serve.

LELA'S BROWNIES

⅓ cup butter or oleo
¾ cup sugar
¼ cup corn syrup or ½ cup honey
2 teaspoons vanilla
2 eggs
½ cup flour
⅓ cup cocoa
½ teaspoon salt
1 cup nuts, chopped

Preheat oven to 350°. Cream together butter and sugar. Blend in syrup or honey and vanilla. Add eggs one at a at a time beating well after each. Combine flour, cocoa, and salt. Gradually add to creamed mixture. Stir in nuts. Pour into greased 9x9x1¾ inch pan. Bake for 25 to 30 minutes. Frost with chocolate icing if desired.

TAN BROWNIES

- 2/3 cup butter or oleo, melted
- 2 cups brown sugar
- 2 eggs
- 1 teaspoon vanilla
- 2 cups flour
- 1 teaspoon baking powder
- 1/2 teaspoon soda
- 1/2 teaspoon salt
- 1/2 cup pecans, chopped
- 1 5 3/4 ounce package milk chocolate chips

Preheat oven to 350°. Combine butter, sugar, eggs and vanilla, beat well. Combine dry ingredients, add to sugar mixture, blend well. Stir in nuts. Spread in 13x9x2 inch pan. Sprinkle with chocolate chips. Bake for 25 to 30 minutes. Cool. Cut into squares. Makes 30.

BISCUIT PUFFS

- 1 10 ounce can biscuits
- 1/2 cup raisins, chopped
- 1/2 cup nuts, chopped
- 1/2 teaspoon cinnamon
- 1/2 cup sugar
- 3 tablespoons butter or oleo, melted

Preheat oven to 375°. Separate biscuits into 10 biscuits, press each into 4 inch circle. Mix raisins and nuts, press each biscuit firmly into fruit mixture. Shape each into ball with fruit inside. Seal well. Place seam side down on ungreased cookie sheet. Bake for 10 to 12 minutes. Combine sugar and cinnamon in paper bag. Dip hot puffs in melted butter, shake in sugar mixture. Serve warm. Makes 10.

BLACK WALNUT BALLS

- 1/2 cup butter or oleo
- 1/2 cup powdered sugar, sifted
- 1/8 teaspoon salt
- 1 tablespoon brandy
- 1/2 teaspoon vanilla
- 1 cup flour, sifted
- 1/2 cup black walnuts, finely chopped
- Powdered sugar

Preheat oven to 325°. Cream butter, sugar and salt til fluffy. Stir in brandy and vanilla. Stir in flour and nuts, mix well. Shape into 3/4 inch balls. Place on ungreased cookie sheet. Bake for 20 minutes. Roll in powdered sugar. Makes 36.

MEXICAN MOCHA COOKIES

1 cup butter or oleo
½ cup sugar
1 teaspoon vanilla
2 cups flour
¼ cup cocoa powder
1 teaspoon instant coffee
¼ teaspoon salt
1 cup nuts, chopped
½ cup maraschino cherries, chopped
Fine granulated sugar

Preheat oven to 325°. In bowl cream butter, sugar and vanilla til fluffy. Stir together flour, cocoa powder, coffee powder and salt. Gradually beat into creamed mixture. Stir in nuts and cherries. Chill dough 1 hour. Shape into 1 inch balls. Place on cookie sheet. Bake for 20 minutes. Cool on rack. While warm, but not hot, dust with fine granulated sugar.

ALMOND SPICE BARS

1 cup brown sugar
1 cup butter or oleo, softened
1 egg yolk
1 teaspoon vanilla
2 cups flour
⅛ teaspoon salt
1 egg white, slightly beaten
¼ cup sugar
½ teaspoon cinnamon
½ cup almonds, sliced

Preheat oven to 350°. Cream butter and sugar til fluffy, beat in egg yolk and vanilla. Stir together flour and salt, blend into creamed mixture, mixing well. Pat dough in ungreased 15x10x1 inch pan. Brush top of dough with egg white. Combine sugar and cinnamon, sprinkle over dough. Sprinkle with almonds. Bake for 15 minutes. Cut into diamonds while warm. Makes 48.

APPLESAUCE BARS

2 cups flour
1 teaspoon baking soda
¾ teaspoon cinnamon
¼ teaspoon nutmeg
½ cup butter or oleo, softened
1 cup sugar
2 eggs
1 teaspoon vanilla
1½ cups applesauce
1 cup pecans, chopped
1 cup raisins
Powdered sugar

Preheat oven to 350°. Mix flour with soda and spices. Cream butter and sugar til fluffy. Add eggs and vanilla, beat well. Stir in dry ingredients. Add applesauce, nuts and raisins, stir til blended. Pour into greased 15x10x1 inch pan. Bake for 25 minutes. Cool. Cut into bars, sprinkle with powdered sugar. Makes 56.

BROWN SUGAR BARS

- 2 tablespoons butter or oleo
- 1 cup brown sugar
- 5 tablespoons flour
- ⅛ teaspoon soda
- 1 cup nuts, chopped
- 2 eggs, beaten
- 1 teaspoon vanilla
- Powdered sugar

Preheat oven to 350°. In 8 inch square pan melt butter. Combine remaining ingredients, mix well. Pour over butter, do not stir. Bake for 25 to 30 minutes. Cool slightly, sprinkle with powdered sugar. Cut into bars. Makes 18.

CHOCOLATE BARS

- 1 cup butter or oleo
- 2 cups brown sugar
- 2 eggs
- 2 teaspoons vanilla
- 2½ cups flour, sifted
- 1 teaspoon baking soda
- 1 teaspoon salt
- 3 cups quick cooking rolled oats
- 1 15 ounce can sweetened condensed milk
- 1 12 ounce package semisweet chocolate chips
- 2 tablespoons butter or oleo
- ½ teaspoon salt
- 1 cup walnuts, chopped
- 2 teaspoons vanilla

Preheat oven to 350°. In large bowl, cream together the butter and brown sugar. Beat in eggs and 2 teaspoons vanilla. Sift together flour, soda and 1 teaspoon salt, stir in oats. Stir dry ingredients into creamed mixture, set aside. in saucepan melt together milk, chocolate chips, rest of butter and salt over low heat, stirring til smooth. Stir in nuts and remaining vanilla. Pat ⅔ oat mixture in bottom of 15x10x1 inch pan. Spread chocolate mixture over. Dot with rest of oat mixture. Bake for 25 to 30 minutes. Cool. Cut into 2x1 inch bars. Makes 75.

CHOCOLATE COCONUT BARS

- 1 cup brown sugar
- ½ cup butter or oleo, softened
- 2 cups rolled oats
- 1 cup coconut, grated
- 1½ teaspoons instant coffee
- 2 squares semisweet chocolate
- 1 tablespoon shortening

Preheat oven to 350°. In bowl combine sugar, butter, oats, coconut and instant coffee, mix well. Press into lightly greased 11x7x2 inch pan. Bake for 30 minutes. Cool on rack. Cut into 24 bars. Melt chocolate and shortening together, drizzle on cookies. Refrigerate to harden. Makes 24.

DOUBLE NUT BARS

- ½ cup butter or oleo, melted
- 1½ cups graham cracker crumbs
- 1 cup walnuts, chopped
- 1 cup (6 ounce package) semi sweet chocolate chips
- 1⅓ cups coconut, grated
- 1 15 ounce can sweetened condensed milk

Preheat oven to 350°. Pour melted butter into 13x9x2 inch pan. Sprinkle crumbs over. Sprinkle nuts over crumbs. Scatter chocolate chips over nuts. Sprinkle coconut over chips. Pour milk over coconut. Bake for 25 minutes. Cool in pan 15 minutes. Cut into bars. Makes 24.

LAYERED COOKIES

- ½ cup sugar
- ½ cup butter or oleo
- 1 egg yolk
- ½ cup almonds, ground
- ½ teaspoon lemon peel, grated
- ¾ cup flour
- ¼ teaspoon salt
- ¼ teaspoon cinnamon
- 1 beaten egg white
- 2 tablespoons almonds, chopped
- ⅓ cup red currant jelly

Preheat oven to 350°. In large bowl cream sugar and butter til fluffy. Beat in egg yolk. Stir in ½ cup almonds and lemon peel. Stir together dry ingredients, stir into creamed mixture. Divide dough in half. Pat each half into bottoms of 2 greased 8x8x2 inch pans. Brush one pan with egg white, sprinkle with almonds. Bake both for 18 to 20 minutes. Cool 3 minutes. Invert pans to remove layers, spread jelly over unglazed square. Place the other square, nut side up, on top of jelly. While warm, cut into squares. An electric knife makes it simple. Makes 16.

MAGIC COOKIE BARS

- ½ cup butter or oleo, melted
- 1½ cups graham cracker crumbs
- 1 can sweetened condensed milk
- 1 6 ounce package chocolate chips
- 1 3½ ounce can coconut, flaked
- 1 cup nuts, chopped

Preheat oven to 350°. Put melted butter in 13x9 inch pan, sprinkle with crumbs. Pour milk evenly over crumbs, sprinkle with chips, coconut and nuts. Press down gently. Bake for 25 to 30 minutes. Cool. Cut into bars. Makes 24.

PARTY PRUNE BARS

½ cup frozen lemonade concentrate, thawed
1 cup pitted prunes
½ cup brown sugar
2 tablespoons flour
⅛ teaspoon salt
½ cup walnuts, chopped
1 cup flour
1 cup quick cooking oats
½ cup brown sugar
½ teaspoon cinnamon
½ cup butter or oleo

Preheat oven to 350°. Add water to lemonade to make 1 cup. In saucepan simmer prunes, covered, in lemonade til tender, about 5 minutes. Combine the ½ cup brown sugar, 2 tablespoons flour, salt and walnuts, add to prune mixture. Cook, stirring constantly, til mixture thickens, about 5 minutes. Cool. Combine the 1 cup flour, oats, ½ cup brown sugar and cinnamon. Cut in butter, mixing well. Pat half of oat mixture in bottom of greased 9x9x2 inch pan. Spread prune mixture over. Crumble remaining mixture on top pressing lightly into prune mixture. Bake for 30 to 35 minutes. Cool. Cut into squares. Makes 24.

PECAN BARS

1 cup butter or oleo, softened
1 cup sugar
1 egg, separated
2 cups flour
2 teaspoons cinnamon
1 tablespoon milk
1 cup pecans, chopped

Preheat oven to 350°. Cream together butter and sugar, add egg yolk, beating well. Add flour, cinnamon and milk, mix well. Pat dough evenly in greased 13x9x2 inch pan. Beat egg white slightly, brush over top of dough, sprinkle with pecans. Press pecans lightly into dough. Bake for 35 to 45 minutes. Cut into bars while hot. Makes 30.

PECAN PIE BARS

1 package yellow cake mix
½ cup butter or oleo, melted
4 eggs, divided
½ cup brown sugar
1½ cups dark corn syrup
1 teaspoon vanilla
1 cup pecans, chopped

Preheat oven to 350°. Set aside ⅔ cup cake mix. In bowl combine rest of cake mix, butter and 1 egg. Mix with fork til crumbly. Press crumbs into greased 13x9x2 inch pan. Bake for 15 to 20 minutes. Combine rest of cake mix, 3 eggs, brown sugar, corn syrup and vanilla, beat at medium speed 1 to 2 minutes. Pour over crust, sprinkle with pecans. Bake for 30 to 35 minutes. Cool. Cut into bars. Makes 36 to 48.

SOUTHERN FRUIT BARS

¼ cup shortening
½ cup sugar
1 egg
½ cup molasses
2 cups flour
¼ teaspoon salt
¼ teaspoon soda
1½ teaspoons baking powder
½ cup milk
1 cup pecans or walnuts, chopped
1 cup dates, chopped (or raisins)

Preheat oven to 350°. Cream shortening and sugar til fluffy. Add egg and molasses, blend well. Combine dry ingredients, add to creamed mixture alternating with milk. Beat well after each addition. Stir in nuts and dates. Spread batter in greased 12x8x2 inch pan. Bake for 30 minutes. Cool. Cut into bars. Makes 48.

NO BAKE CHINESE HAY STACKS

1 6 ounce package Butterscotch chips
1 cup chunky peanut butter
2 3 ounce cans Chow Mein noodles

In heavy saucepan heat peanut butter and butterscotch chips. When chips are dissolved add noodles. Drop by teaspoon on wax paper.

NO BAKE CHOCOLATE NUTTIES

1 8 ounce Hershey Bar with almonds
2 cups corn flakes
1 cup pecans, whole or chopped
1 square unsweetened chocolate

In top of double boiler melt Hershey bar and chocolate square, blend well. Remove from heat, stir in corn flakes and nuts. Stir til chocolate coats all ingredients. Drop by teaspoonsfuls onto wax paper. Refrigerate for 30 minutes. Keep in cool place.

Candy

Candy

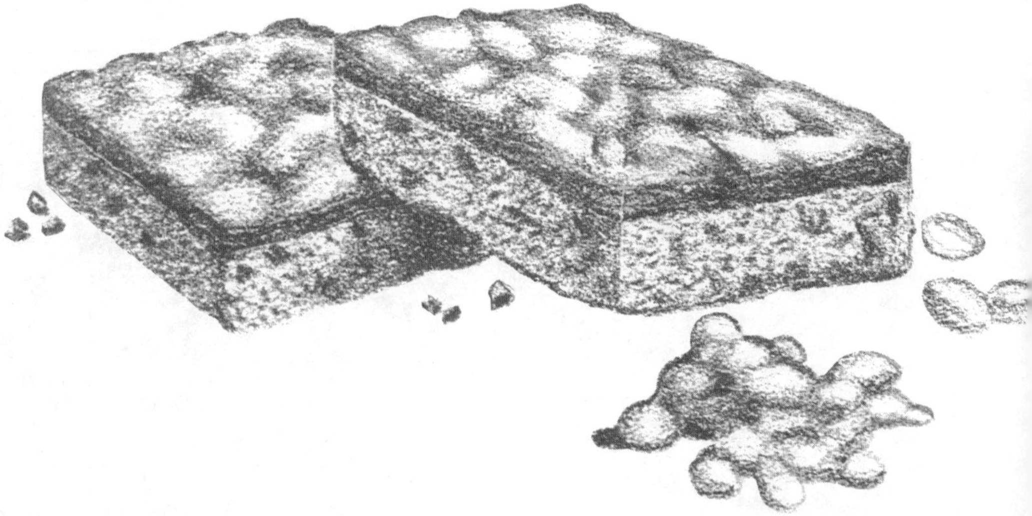

MARZIPAN

- 2⅔ cups blanched almonds
- 2 egg whites, slightly beaten
- 2 teaspoons almond extract
- 4½ cups powdered sugar, sifted
- 2 to 4 tablespoons orange juice

Grind almonds in blender. Combine almonds, egg whites, extract and sugar. Add juice 1 tablespoon at a time til mixture is easy to handle. Knead til smooth. Form into desired shapes—fruits, flowers, vegetables—using hands or small molds. Let dry on wax paper. Color with food coloring diluted with a little water. Allow to dry. Refrigerate.

NEW ORLEANS PRALINES

- 3 cups sugar
- 1 teaspoon baking soda
- ⅛ teaspoon salt
- 1 cup buttermilk
- ¾ cup corn syrup
- 2 tablespoons butter or oleo
- 2 cups pecan halves

In large saucepan combine sugar, baking soda and salt. Stir in buttermilk and corn syrup. Over medium heat, bring to boil, stirring constantly. Cook and stir til 234° on candy thermometer. Remove from heat, add butter. Stir in pecans, beat til mixture is thick enough to drop from spoon, 5 to 6 minutes. Quickly drop from tablespoon onto wax paper. If candy becomes too stiff, add 1 teaspoon hot water. Makes 45 pralines.

ORANGE CANDY

- 2 cups sugar
- Dash salt
- 4 tablespoons corn syrup
- ¾ cup evaporated milk
- Juice of 1 orange
- Peel of ½ orange, grated
- ½ stick butter or oleo
- 1 teaspoon vanilla
- 1 cup pecans, slightly toasted

Bring sugar, salt, syrup and milk to boil. Add orange juice, cook to 234° on candy thermometer. Add peel, cook to 250°. Cool. Add butter, vanilla and nuts. Beat, drop by teaspoonfuls onto greased cookie sheet. Store in airtight container.

CANDY

ALMOND CHOCOLATE KISSES

1 cup sugar
1 cup dark corn syrup
½ cup water
½ cup light cream
¼ teaspoon salt
¼ cup butter or oleo
4 squares unsweetened chocolate
1 teaspoon vanilla
1 cup unblanched almonds, toasted

In large saucepan bring sugar, syrup, water, cream and salt to boil. Boil 5 minutes. Add butter, cook gently, stirring occasionally, to 230° on candy thermometer. Add chocolate, bring to boil and cook, stirring occasionally, to 240° on candy thermometer. Remove from heat, stir in vanilla. Pour into buttered 9 inch pan. Cool completely. Lift from pan, cut into 64 squares. Put 2 almonds in center of each square. With fingers shape into oblong shape, covering nuts. Wrap each piece in wax paper. Store in airtight tins.

ICED ALMONDS

2 cups whole blanched almonds
1 cup sugar
4 tablespoons butter or oleo
1 teaspoon vanilla

In heavy skillet heat nuts, sugar and butter over medium heat, stirring constantly, til almonds are toasted and sugar is golden brown, about 15 minutes. Stir in vanilla. Drop by teaspoonfuls onto cookie sheet, sprinkle with a little salt. Cool.

APRICOT CANDY ROLL

2 cups sugar
1 cup milk
12 ounces dried apricots, chopped
1 tablespoon butter or oleo
2 cups pecans, chopped
1 teaspoon vanilla
Dash salt

Boil sugar and milk til 236° on candy thermometer, stirring constantly. Add apricots, boil til they melt into syrup and mixture reaches 230° on candy thermometer. Remove from heat, beat hard. Add butter, pecans, vanilla and salt. Beat candy til it begins to harden. Pour into wet, smooth cloth and roll into desired diameter. Cool. Store in refrigerator. To serve cut into thin slices.

BRAZIL NUT FUDGE

2 cups sugar
1 cup maple syrup
½ cup milk
2 squares unsweetened chocolate, cut up
Dash salt
2 tablespoons butter or oleo
1 teaspoon vanilla
1 cup Brazil nuts, chopped

In large saucepan combine sugar, syrup, milk, chocolate and salt. Cook over medium heat til sugar dissolves. Bring to boil, cook to 236° on candy thermometer, stirring occasionally. Remove pan from heat, add butter, cool without stirring to 110° on candy thermometer. Add vanilla. Beat vigorously about 10 minutes. Beat in nuts. Pour into large buttered pan. Cut into squares. Store at room temperature.

BUTTER CRUNCH

1 cup sugar
½ cup butter or oleo
¼ cup water
½ teaspoon salt
1 cup chocolate chips
⅔ cup nuts, chopped

In saucepan combine sugar, butter, water and salt, stirring constantly, over low heat, til sugar is dissolved. Cook til mixture reaches 285° on candy thermometer. Pour into buttered 9 inch square pan. Cool. Melt chocolate and spread half over cooled mixture. Sprinkle with half the nuts, pressing them into chocolate. Turn candy over and repeat with remaining chocolate and nuts. Break into pieces.

CARAMELIZED FRUIT AND NUTS

1 cup brown sugar
½ cup granulated sugar
½ cup milk
1 tablespoon corn syrup
1 tablespoon butter or oleo
½ cup walnut halves
½ cup pecan halves
¼ cup whole blanched almonds, toasted
¼ cup pitted dates, chopped
¼ cup candied cherries, chopped

In saucepan combine brown sugar, granulated sugar, milk and syrup. Cook and stir over medium heat til sugars dissolve and mixture boils. Cool to 236°. Add butter and vanilla. Let cool several minutes. Beat just til mixture begins to lose its gloss, 3 to 5 minutes. Quickly stir in nuts and fruits til coated. Immediately drop by teaspoonfuls onto buttered cookie sheet.

CANDY

CARMELITAS

1 roll refrigerated chocolate chip cookie dough
1 cup semisweet chocolate chips
32 vanilla caramels
¼ cup evaporated milk
Pecan halves

Preheat oven to 375°. Slice dough into ¼ inch rounds, place on bottom of 9x9x2 inch pan, pat to make even. Bake for 25 minutes. Cool slightly. Sprinkle chocolate chips over. In top of double boiler melt caramels in milk, stirring til smooth. Carefully spread atop chips. Refrigerate 1 to 2 hours. Cut into 1 inch squares. Top each with pecan half.

CHRISTMAS CANDY

3 cups sugar
1 cup corn syrup
1½ cups light cream
½ pound candied pineapple, chunked
½ pound black walnuts, chopped
½ pound Brazil nuts, chopped
½ pound pecans, chopped
1 teaspoon vanilla
½ pound candied cherries, chopped

In heavy saucepan cook sugar, syrup and cream to 248° on candy thermometer, stirring constantly. Remove from heat. Beat til mixture begins to thicken. Add nuts, fruits and vanilla. Mix well. Pour into buttered 10x15 inch pan. Cool. Cut into squares.

CHOCOLATE COCONUT TIDBITS

1 12 ounce package semisweet chocolate chips
1 cup coconut, grated
¾ cup toasted almonds, finely chopped

In top of double boiler, melt chocolate. Add coconut and ½ cup nuts, mix well. Drop in clusters into candy cups. Sprinkle with remaining nuts. Store in cool dry place.

CHOCOLATE PEANUT CANDY

1 12 ounce package chocolate chips
1 can sweetened condensed milk
2 cups Rice Krispies
1 cup peanuts

In top of double boiler melt chocolate chips, stir in milk. Remove from heat, stir in Rice Krispies and peanuts. Drop by teaspoons onto wax paper lined cookie sheets. Chill til firm. Store at room temperature in loosely covered container.

CREME DE MENTHE BALLS

2½ cups vanilla wafer crumbs
1 cup powdered sugar, sifted
2 tablespoons cocoa
1 cup walnuts, finely chopped
¼ cup corn syrup
¼ cup white creme de menthe
Granulated sugar

Combine crumbs, powdered sugar, cocoa, and nuts. Stir in syrup and creme de menthe. If too stiff add a few drops water. Form into 1 inch balls. Roll in granulated sugar. Store in airtight tin.

CRUNCHY CARAMEL CORN

3 quarts popcorn, popped
1½ cups almonds, slivered
1½ cups pecan halves
½ cup butter or oleo
1 cup brown sugar
¼ cup honey
1 teaspoon vanilla

Preheat oven to 250°. Combine popcorn and nuts in greased oblong pan. Mix well and set aside. In saucepan melt margarine and add brown sugar and honey. Boil 5 minutes without stirring. Add vanilla and stir well. Pour over popcorn mixture and stir til evenly coated. Bake for 1 hour stirring every 15 minutes. Cool completely then break into pieces. Store in airtight container.

CANDY

DATE NUT ROLL CANDY

1 pound graham crackers, crushed
1 medium bottle maraschino cherries, chopped
2 cups pecans, chopped
1 pound dates, chopped
1 cup raisins
1 cup coconut, grated
2/3 cup evaporated milk
1 pound bag marshmallows

Mix crumbs with fruit and nuts. In top of double boiler melt marshmallows in milk, stirring often. Pour over dry ingredients. Mix with hands. Roll in wax paper to make logs. Wrap in foil and refrigerate. Slice to serve. Keeps indefinitely.

DIVINITY

1 cup boiling water
3/4 cup corn syrup
3 cups sugar
Pinch salt
2 egg whites
1 cup pecans, chopped
1 teaspoon vanilla

Combine water, syrup, sugar and salt, cook to 234° on candy thermometer. Add 1/2 of the syrup, 1 tablespoon at a time, to well-beaten egg whites, beating constantly. Continue cooking other 1/2 of syrup til it reaches 270°. Pour into egg mixture, beat til high gloss changes to dull. Fold in pecans and vanilla, drop by teaspoonful onto wax paper. Makes 48.

EUROPEAN NUT CANDY

1 cup sugar
1 cup pecans, chopped
1 teaspoon vanilla
1/8 teaspoon salt

In 10 inch skillet heat and stir sugar til melted and golden brown. Stir in pecans, vanilla and salt. Pour onto buttered baking sheet. Roll quickly with buttered rolling pin to 8x8x1/4 inch square. Quickly cut into squares or break into small pieces.

FILBERT CLUSTERS

1 12 ounce package semisweet chocolate chips
¼ teaspoon salt
1½ cups toasted filberts, finely chopped
1½ cups golden raisins

In top of double boiler, melt chocolate, cool to lukewarm. Add remaining ingredients, blend thoroughly. Drop in clusters into paper candy cups. Cover lightly with plastic wrap. Store in cool place to harden.

FRENCH FUDGE

3 6 ounce packages semi-sweet chocolate chips
2 cans sweetened condensed milk
1½ teaspoons vanilla
½ cup nuts, chopped
Dash salt

In top of double boiler melt chocolate chips, remove from heat. Add remaining ingredients, stir in smooth. Pour into buttered 8x8 inch pan. Chill 2 hours. Cut into squares.

MAMA B'S FUDGE

2 cups sugar
1 small can evaporated milk
1 stick butter or oleo
1 cup Nestles chocolate chips
26 marshmallows
1 teaspoon vanilla
½ cup pecans, chopped

Melt marshmallows in top of double boiler. In medium saucepan combine sugar, milk and butter. Over medium heat melt butter then let mixture come to full boil, stirring constantly. Boil 5 minutes, stirring constantly. Remove from heat, add chocolate chips and marshmallows, beat til all is melted. Stir in vanilla and nuts. Pour into buttered 8 inch square pan. Refrigerate about 30 minutes. Cut, then return to refrigerator til hard.

CANDY

NUTRITIOUS FUDGE

1 cup honey
1 cup peanut butter
1 cup carob powder
1 cup sunflower seeds, shelled
½ cup sesame seed, toasted
½ cup coconut, grated
½ cup walnuts, chopped
½ cup raisins

In large saucepan, heat honey and peanut butter, stirring constantly til smooth. Remove from heat, stir in carob powder, mix well. Add remaining ingredients. Press into buttered 8x8x2 inch pan. Chill several hours. Cut into 1 inch squares. Keep refrigerated.

FUDGE-NUT BON BONS

½ cup butter or oleo, softened
1 cup powdered sugar
⅔ cup cocoa powder
1 cup coconut, grated
1 cup golden raisins
1 cup walnuts, chopped
2 tablespoons brandy
1 egg white, unbeaten

Beat butter til creamy. Sift powdered sugar and cocoa. Gradually beat into butter. Add ⅔ cup coconut, raisins, nuts and brandy, mix well. Beat in egg white. Let stand in refrigerator 30 minutes, shape into small balls, roll in coconut. Store in refrigerator.

GOODY! GOODY!

4 sticks butter or oleo
2 boxes powdered sugar
1 quart crunchy peanut butter
1 cup pecans, ground
2½ 6 ounce packages semi-sweet chocolate chips
1 block paraffin

In bowl mix butter, sugar, peanut butter and nuts. Roll into 1 inch balls. Chill til firm. In double boiler melt paraffin and chocolate chips. Insert toothpick into ball, dip into hot chocolate mixture. Remove toothpick, set on wax paper. Let cool.

HOLIDAY DELIGHT

3 cups sugar
1 cup corn syrup
1½ cups light cream
1½ teaspoons vanilla
1 cup Brazil nuts, cut in half
2 cups pecan halves
1 cup black walnuts, chopped
½ pound candied red cherries, cut in half
½ pound green candied pineapple, cut in wedges

Combine sugar, corn syrup, and cream, cook to 238° over medium heat. Remove from heat, beat immediately. Mixture will thicken and begin to change color. Add vanilla, continue beating. Add nuts and fruits slowly to mixture. Pack into loaf pan lined with wax paper, pressing down firmly with wet spoon. Chill in refrigerator. Slice after 24 hours. Candy keeps for several months.

PATIENCE

4 cups sugar
1 cup milk
1 teaspoon salt
2 cups nuts, chopped
2 tablespoons butter or oleo

In saucepan caramelize 1 cup sugar. Place 3 cups sugar and milk in another saucepan and cook over low heat. Slowly add caramelized sugar to sugar and milk mixture in saucepan stirring constantly. Cook until mixture reaches 236° on candy thermometer. Remove from heat and add salt, nuts, and 2 tablespoons butter. Beat until creamy. Pour into buttered pan to cool. Cut into squares.

PEANUT BUTTER POPCORN BALLS

6 cups popped corn
½ cup sugar
½ cup corn syrup
½ cup peanut butter
½ teaspoon vanilla

Lightly salt popcorn, keep warm. In saucepan combine sugar and syrup, cook and stir over medium heat just til mixture comes to full rolling boil, 3 to 4 minutes. Remove from heat, stir in peanut butter and vanilla. Immediately pour over warm popcorn, mixing gently til all is coated. With buttered hands form into balls. Wrap in clear plastic wrap or wax paper. Makes 8 to 10 balls.

CANDY

PEANUT BRITTLE

2 cups granulated sugar
2 cups shelled skinned peanuts, coarsely chopped

In heavy skillet heat sugar over moderate heat, stirring constantly, til it becomes brown syrup. Add nuts and blend. Pour at once onto buttered platter. Mark out squares when soft and break into pieces when cold and hard. Store in airtight container between pieces of waxed paper. Peanut brittle may be eaten as candy, or crushed or ground to a powder and used as flavoring for creams, custards and puddings. To crush put through a meat grinder or spread on several thicknesses of wax paper and roll with rolling pin. Store tightly covered in glass jar in cool place.

PECAN GOODIES

1 cup pecan pieces
1 6 ounce package chocolate chips
½ cup sugar
½ cup evaporated milk
1 tablespoon corn syrup

In saucepan boil sugar, milk and corn syrup 2 minutes. Stir in chocolate chips and pecans. Drop by teaspoonful onto wax paper. Let cool.

PECAN KISSES

1 egg white, beaten stiff
1 teaspoon vanilla
¾ cup brown sugar
2 cups pecan halves

Preheat oven to 250°. Gradually add brown sugar and vanilla to egg whites. Fold in pecans and coat well. Drop by teaspoonful 1 inch apart on greased cookie sheet. Bake for 30 minutes. Turn off oven and let stay 30 more minutes.

PISTACHIO NUT LAYERS

½ cup butter or oleo
1 3½ ounce package instant pistachio pudding mix
3 tablespoons milk
2 cups powdered sugar, sifted
1 6 ounce package semisweet chocolate chips
2 tablespoons butter or oleo
1 8 ounce cream cheese, cubed and softened
1 teaspoon vanilla
1 cup powdered sugar, sifted
1 cup Cool Whip
½ cup pistachios, chopped (or walnuts)

Beat butter til light, beat in dry pudding mix and milk. Gradually beat in 2 cups powdered sugar til fluffy. Spread in 11x7x2 inch pan. Chill til firm. In heavy saucepan melt chocolate chips and 2 tablespoons butter over low heat. Remove, blend in cream cheese and vanilla, stir in remaining 1 cup powdered sugar. Fold in Cool Whip. Spread on pudding layer. Freeze til firm. Cut into 1 inch squares. Dip in nuts and coat bottom and sides of chocolate layer. Store in refrigerator.

ROCKY ROAD

2 8 ounce milk chocolate candy bars
3 cups miniature marshmallows
¾ cup nuts, chopped

In saucepan melt chocolate over low heat, stirring constantly. Remove from heat, beat smooth. Stir in marshmallows and nuts. Spread in buttered 8x8x2 inch pan. Chill. Cut into squares.

RUM BALLS

2 cups vanilla wafer crumbs
½ cup rum
½ cup honey
4 cups walnuts, ground
Powdered sugar

Mix together crumbs, rum, honey and nuts. Shape into balls, roll in powdered sugar. Store in airtight tin. Will last in tin up to 6 weeks.

STRAWBERRY GEMS

- 1 can sweetened condensed milk
- 4 3½ ounce cans coconut
- ⅓ cup strawberry Jello
- 1 cup blanched almonds, ground
- 1 teaspoon almond extract
- Red food coloring

In large bowl combine milk, coconut, Jello, nuts and flavorings. Add enough food coloring to tint mixture a strawberry shade. Chill til firm enough to handle. Form about ½ teaspoonful at a time into strawberry shapes. Sprinkle remainder of Jello onto flat dish, roll each strawberry to coat. Make stem with green decorator icing. Place on cookie sheet. Refrigerate.

STUFFED FIGS

- 1 12 ounce package dried whole figs
- 1 cup orange juice
- 1 tablespoon lemon peel, grated
- 1 tablespoon lemon juice
- 3 tablespoons sugar
- 24 pecan halves
- Granulated sugar

Remove stem end from figs. Combine figs, orange juice, lemon peel and lemon juice, pour over figs in saucepan, heat to boiling. Simmer, covered, til fruit is tender, about 45 minutes. Drain well. Cool. Insert knife in stem end of each fig to form pocket. Fill each pocket with pecan half. Roll figs in sugar. Let dry overnight.

TOFFEE

- 1 cup sugar
- 1 cup dark corn syrup
- 1 cup heavy cream
- ½ cup almonds, chopped
- ¼ teaspoon baking powder

In large saucepan combine sugar, syrup and cream. Cook over low heat 50 minutes, stirring occasionally, or til mixture reaches 246° on candy thermometer. Add almonds and baking powder, mix well. Spoon into paper candy cups. Let stand at room temperature til firm. Store in cool place.

TOFFEE CRUNCH

1 cup butter or oleo
1½ cups sugar
3 tablespoons water
1 tablespoon corn syrup
½ cup almonds, coarsely chopped
1 4½ ounce milk chocolate candy bar
1 inch square paraffin
½ cup toasted almonds, finely chopped

In large saucepan, melt butter, add sugar, water and corn syrup. Cook over medium heat, stirring often. Cook to 300° on candy thermometer. Quickly stir in nuts. Spread in foil-lined 13x9x2 inch pan. Cool thoroughly. Turn out onto wax paper. Melt together chocolate and paraffin. Spread over candy, sprinkle with finely chopped nuts. Chill to firm chocolate. Cut into irregular pieces.

TURTLES

40 Kraft caramels
¼ cup corn syrup
3 tablespoons water
2½ cups pecans
¼ cup paraffin
1 8 ounce Hershey bar

Put caramels, syrup and water in pan over medium heat, sitrring constantly til caramels melt. Add nuts, mix well. Drop by teaspoonful onto greased cookie sheet, let cool. In top of double boiler melt paraffin. Add candy bar, stir til smooth. With toothpicks dip clusters into paraffin mixture til covered. Put on wax paper.

MICROWAVE PEANUT TREATS

1 12 ounce package caramels
2 tablespoons water
1 cup salted peanuts
8 cups Rice Krispies

Place caramels and water in quart casserole, cook in microwave for 6 minutes til caramels melt. Stir til mixture is smooth. Stir in peanuts. Pour mixture over Rice Krispies. Press mixture into buttered oblong pan. Cool. Cut into squares. Makes about 40.

MICROWAVE MORSELS

1 package semisweet chocolate chips
Miniature marshmallows
Pecans, walnuts, or almonds, chopped

Put chocolate chips in glass dish, melt on High for 2 minutes. Remove, stir til glossy. Add marshmallows and nuts. Mix well. Spread on wax paper on cookie sheet. Put in freezer til hard. Remove, peel off paper. Break into small pieces.

EASY MICROWAVE FUDGE

1 box powdered sugar
½ cup cocoa
¼ cup milk
1 stick butter or oleo
1 teaspoon vanilla
½ cup pecans, chopped

Place sugar, cocoa, milk and butter in 2 quart glass dish. Cook 3½ minutes. Remove and blend til smooth. Add vanilla and pecans. Blend again. Pour into buttered 8 inch square dish, refrigerate 1 hour or put in freezer for 20 minutes. Cut into squares.

Appendix

APPENDIX

WHAT SIZE CAN SHOULD YOU USE?

To Serve	Product	Size Can	Total Cups
4 to 6 people	Fruits, Vegetables, Juices	No. 2	2½ cups
6 to 8 people	Fruits, Vegetables	No. 2½	3½ cups
6 to 8 people	Juices	46 ozs.	5¾ cups
18 to 25	Fruits, Vegetables	No. 10	13 cups

MAKING THE PERFECT PIE CRUST

A tasty, flaky homemade pie crust is easy to make if you follow these simple instructions:

1. Assemble your ingredients: ⅔ cup lard, 2 cups flour, 3 to 6 tablespoons cold water, and 1 teaspoon salt.

2. Sift flour and salt together and cut lard into this mixture with fork until crumbs are grainy and coarse.

3. Add water a little at a time, blending thoroughly with the flour until the dough holds into a ball.

4. Using half the dough, roll to ⅛-inch thickness. Lifting crust wwith rolling pin, line pie pan, leaving ½ inch of crust to extend over edge of pie pan. If you want a top crust, continue with instructions. If not, crimp edges, fill pie and bake.

5. Fold filling into crust. Make top crust just as you did bottom crust, inly make several gashes in top crust to allow steam to escape. Place over filling allowing top crust to overlap. Fold top crust under lower crust and crimp edges.

APPENDIX

TABLE OF MEASURE

	In Shell	Shelled	Measure
Almonds	1 pound		1 to 1¾ cups
		1 pound	3½ cups
Black walnuts	1 pound		1 cup
		1 pound	2¾ to 3 cups
Brazil nuts	1 pound		1½ cups
		1 pound	3 cups
Butternuts	1 pound		1 cup
		1 pound	3 cups
Chestnuts	1 pound		2½ cups
		1 pound	4 cups
Coconut	1 medium		3 to 4 cups
English walnuts	1 pound		1⅔ cups
		1 pound	4 cups
Filberts (hazelnuts)	1 pound		1½ cups
		1 pound	3½ cups
Hickory nuts	1 pound		1⅓ cups
		1 pound	3 cups
Macadamia nuts	1 pound		1½ cups
		1 pound	3 cups
Peanuts	1 pound		2¼ cups
		1 pound	3 cups
Pecans	1 pound		2¼ cups
		1 pound	4 cups
Pistachios	1 pound		4 cups
		1 pound	5 cups

CAN SIZES	WEIGHT	APPROXIMATE CUPS
8 ounce	8 ounces	1
12 ounce	10½ to 12 ounces	1¼
No. 300	14 to 16 ounces	1¾
No. 303	16 to 17 ounces	2
No. 2	1 pound 4 ounces or	2½
	1 pint 2 fluid ounces	2½
No. 2½	1 pound 13 ounces	3½
Baby Foods	3½ to 8 ounces	
Condensed milk	15 ounces	1⅓
Evaporated milk	6 ounces	⅔
	14½ ounces	1⅔

APPENDIX

CAKE TROUBLESHOOTING

PROBLEM	POSSIBLE CAUSE
Cake is bready and solid	Too much flour used
Cake falls	Insufficient quantity of flour or rising ingredients OR excess temperature OR moving cake in the oven before the cell walls have become firm by the heat after the cake has risen.
Uneven surface	Too much heat used
Crusting over the top before mixture has risen to full height	Too much heat used
Bursting at weakest point	Too much heat used
Coarse-grained cakes	Too much leavening ingredients OR too slow an oven OR insufficient creaming of shortening and sugar OR insufficient beating of batter before adding egg whites.
Heavy cakes	Too slow an oven OR too much sugar or shortening.
Heavy streak at bottom of a loaf cake	Too many egg yolks in proportion to other ingredients OR too slow an oven.

TABLE OF EQUIVALENTS AND SUBSTITUTIONS

Apples	1 pound unpared	= 3 cups, pared and sliced
Apples	3 pounds	= 2 quarts, sliced
Baking powder	1 teaspoon single-acting	= ¾ teaspoon double-acting
Baking powder	1 teaspoon double-acting	= ⅓ teaspoon baking soda plus ½ teaspoon cream of tartar
Bananas	1 pound	= 3 to 4 medium sized
Bread crumbs, dry	1 slice	= ⅓ cup
Bread crumbs, soft	1 slice	= ¾ cup
Butter	1 stick	= 8 tablespoons or ½ cup
Butter	1 pound	= 2 cups or 4 sticks
Butter	1 cup	= 1 cups oleo
Buttermilk	1 cup	= 1 cup yogurt
Cheese, grated	1 pound	= 5 cups
Cherries, candied	1 pound	= 3 cups
Chocolate	1 square	= 3 tablespoons cocoa plus 1 tablespoon fat
Chocolate	1 square	= 4 tablespoons, grated
Cocoa	1 pound	= 4 cups
Coconut, grated	3½ ounce	= 1 cup
Coconut	1 pound	= 5 cups shredded
Coconut milk	1 cup	= 1 cup milk
Coconut cream	1 cup	= 1 cup cream
Cornstarch	1 tablespoon	= 2 tablespoons flour
Cracker crumbs	¾ cup	= 1 cup bread crumbs
Cracker, graham	3 cups crumbs	= 30 to 36 crackers
Cracker, salted	1 cup crumbs	= 20 crackers
Cream, sour	1 cup	= 3 tablespoons butter plus ⅞ cup sour milk
Cream, Whipping	1 cup	= 2 to 2½ cups whipped
Dates	1 pound	= 2½ cups pitted
Eggs		
Whole	1 egg	= about 3 tablespoons
	1 cup	= 5 to 6 eggs
Whites	1 white	= about 2 tablespoons
	1 cup	= 8 to 10 whites
Yolks	1 yolk	= about 1 tablespoon
	1 cup	= 14 to 16 yolks
Figs	1 pound	= 2⅔ cups chopped

APPENDIX

Flour, unsifted	1 pound	= 3 cups
All purpose, sifted once	1 pound	= 3¾ cups
Cake	1 pound	= 2 cups
Cake	1 cup sifted	= ⅞ cup sifted all-purpose or 1 cup less 2 tablespoons
Whole-Wheat	1 pound	= 3¾ to 4 cups
Flour, for thickening	1 tablespoon	= 1½ teaspoons cornstarch
Garlic	1 small clove	= ⅛ teaspoon powder
Gelatin	1 envelope	= 1 tablespoon
Herbs	1 tablespoon fresh	= ⅓ to ½ teaspoon dried
Honey		
In breads and rolls	1 cup	= 1 cup sugar
In cakes and cookies	⅞ cup honey but reduce liquid in recipe by 3 tablespoons for each cup honey	= 1 cup sugar
Lemon	1 average	= 2 to 3 tablespoons juice, 2 teaspoons rind
Macaroni	1 cup uncooked	= 2 to 2¼ cups cooked
Marshmallows	½ pound	= 30 standard size
	1 standard size	= 10 miniature
Milk	1 cup	= ½ cup evaporated plus ½ cup water
Milk	1 cup	= 4 tablespoons powdered milk plus 1 cup water
To sour	1 cup sweet milk	= Add 1 tablespoon vinegar or lemon juice to 1 cup minus 1 tablespoon lukewarm milk. Let stand 5 minutes.
Mushrooms	1 pound fresh	= 6 ounce canned
	½ pound sliced raw	= 2½ cups raw
Noodles	1 cup uncooked	= 1¾ cups cooked
Nuts	See table on page 209	
Orange	1 medium	= 6 to 8 tablespoons juice 2 to 3 tablespoons rind
Peas, dry	1 pound	= 2½ cups
Potatoes	1 pound raw unpeeled	= 2 cups mashed
Prunes, dried	1 pound dried	= 2½ cups
	1 pound cooked	= 4 cups
Raisins	1 pound seeded	= 2½ cups
	1 pound seedless	= 3 cups

Rice	1 pound	= 2½ cups uncooked
	1 cup uncooked	= 3 to 3½ cups cooked
	1 cup pre-cooked	= 2 cups
Rolled oats	1 pound	= 4¾ cups
Saccharin	¼ grain	= 1 teaspoon sugar
Salt	12 ounces	= 1 cup
Spaghetti	1 to 1¼ cups raw	= 2½ cups cooked
Sugar		
Brown, packed	1 pound	= 2⅛ cups
Powdered, sifted	1 pound	= about 4 cups
Granulated	1 pound	= 2⅛ cups
Sugar, in baking	1 cup	= 1 cup molasses plus ¼ to ½ teaspoon soda, omit baking powder
Sugar, brown, packed	1 cup	= 1 cup granulated sugar
Sugar, powdered	1 cup	= 1 cup granulated sugar
Sweetener, liquid	⅛ teaspoon	= 1 teaspoon sugar
Tapioca	2 teaspoons	= 1 tablespoon flour
Vanilla Wafers	1 cup crumbs	= about 22 wafers
Yeast	1 cake yeast	= 1 level tablespoon active dry
	1 package dry yeast	= 1 level tablespoon active dry
Yogurt	1 cup	= 1 cup buttermilk

COOK'S GUIDE

COOKING TERMS

Boil—Cooking in water, or liquid at boiling temperature. Bubbles will rise continually and break on the surface.

Broil—Cooking uncovered by direct heat, placing rack under the source of heat.

Pan-boil—Cooking in lightly greased pan on top of stove. Pour fat off as it accumulates so food does not fry.

Baste—Moistening food while cooking by pouring melted fat, drippings or other liquid over it.

Cream—Mashing or mixing foods together until creamy.

Pan-fry—Cooking in small amount of fat in fry pan.

Knead—Pressing, stretching and folding dough mixture to make it smooth. Bread dough will become elastic.

Parboil—Boiling until partly cooked.

Scald—Heating liquid to just below boiling point.

Simmer—Cooking in liquid just below boiling point. Bubbles will form slowly and break below surface.

Stew—Boiling or simmering in small amount of liquid.

Braise—Cooking slowly in fat and little moisture in closed pot.

HANDY HERB GUIDE

BASIL—Potatoes, cheese, eggs, fish, lamb, tomatoes, peas, squash, duck.

BAY LEAF—Soups, meat stews, tomato sauces and juice.

CHERVIL—Chicken, peas, egg and cheese dishes, spinach, green salads.

CHIVES—Eggs, potatoes, salads, garnish for meats and fish.

DILL—Fish, potatoes, pickles, tomatoes, cream and cottage cheese, fish and vegetable salads.

GARLIC—Meats, vegetables, salads, egg, cheese.

MARJORAM—Vegetable soups, eggs, cheese dishes, beef, lamb, stuffings.

MINT—Beverages, cakes, pies, ice cream, candies, jellies, potatoes.

OREGANO—Tomato sauces, pizza, vegetable salads, chili, pork and veal.

PARSLEY—Meat, vegetables, eggs, cheese, soup.

ROSEMARY—Potatoes, cauliflower, fish, duck, veal, poultry stuffing.

SAGE—Sausages, poultry, hamburgers, pork, stuffings.

SAVORY—Meat, eggs, salads, chicken, soups.

TARRAGON—Vinegar, pickles, chicken, tomatoes, sauces for vegetables and meats, egg and cheese dishes, fish, salads.

THYME—Soups, beef, lamb, veal, pork, oysters, fish, eggs, cheese, stuffings.

APPENDIX

TABLE OF EQUIVALENTS

Standard Equivalents:

A few grains	less than 1/8 teaspoon
1 coffee spoon	1/4 teaspoon
60 drops	1 teaspoon
3 teaspoons	1 tablespoon
2 tablespoons	1 fluid ounce
16 fluid ounces	1 pint
16 ounces	1 pound
16 tablespoons	1 cup
1 cup	1/2 pint
2 pints	1 quart
4 cups	1 quart
4 quarts	1 gallon
8 quarts	1 peck
4 pecks	1 bushel

APPENDIX

METRIC CONVERSIONS

COMMON UNITS OF WEIGHT

1 pound . . . . 454 grams
1 kilogram . . . . 1000 grams or 2.2. pounds
100 grams . . . . $3\frac{1}{3}$ ounces
1 gram . . . . 1/1000 kilogram or .001 kilogram or 1000 milligrams
1 milligram . . . . 1/1000 gram or .001 or 1000 micrograms

COMMON UNITS OF VOLUME

1 quart, 2 pints or 4 cups . . . . 947 milliliters
1 cup, 8 fluid ounces or 16 tablespoons . . . . 237 milliliters
1 fluid ounce . . . . 29.57 milliliters
1 teaspoon . . . . 5 milliliters
1 liter . . . . 1000 milliliters or 1.06 quarts
100 milliliters . . . . $3\frac{1}{3}$ fluid ounces
1 milliliter . . . . 1 cubic centimeter

COMMON UNITS OF LENGTH

1 inch . . . . 2.54 centimeters

COMMON UNITS OF TEMPERATURE

250 degrees fahrenheit . . . . 106 degrees centigrade
350 degrees fahrenheit . . . . 162 degrees centigrade
450 degrees fahrenheit . . . . 218 degrees centigrade

INDEX

A

INDEX

INDEX

INDEX

N

O

INDEX

INDEX

INDEX

W

XYZ

Re-Order Additional Copies

Handy Andy Industries, Inc.
Box 2456
Jonesboro, Arkansas 72401

Please send me ____________ copies of Nuts! Nuts! Nuts! at $8.95 per copy. Add $1.00 per copy for postage. Enclosed is my check ( ) or money order ( ) for $____________.

Make checks payable to Handy Andy Industries, Inc.

Name ____

Street ____

City ________________________ State ________ Zip __________

Handy Andy Industries, Inc.
Box 2456
Jonesboro, Arkansas 72401

Please send me ____________ copies of Nuts! Nuts! Nuts! at $8.95 per copy. Add $1.00 per copy for postage. Enclosed is my check ( ) or money order ( ) for $____________.

Make checks payable to Handy Andy Industries, Inc.

Name ____

Street ____

City ________________________ State ________ Zip __________

Handy Andy Industries, Inc.
Box 2456
Jonesboro, Arkansas 72401

Please send me ____________ copies of Nuts! Nuts! Nuts! at $8.95 per copy. Add $1.00 per copy for postage. Enclosed is my check ( ) or money order ( ) for $____________.

Make checks payable to Handy Andy Industries, Inc.

Name ____

Street ____

City ________________________ State ________ Zip __________